Play
Your Hand

Play Your Hand

Revised Edition

CATHARINE INGRAM

authorHOUSE®

AuthorHouse™
1663 Liberty Drive
Bloomington, IN 47403
www.authorhouse.com
Phone: 1-800-839-8640

Published by AuthorHouse   09/29/2014

ISBN: 978-1-4969-4217-3 (sc)
ISBN: 978-1-4969-4212-8 (e)

Library of Congress Control Number: 2014917161

Chapter 1

It was the first week in May but as the cold wind blew against Frank's back, he thought the weather seemed more appropriate for March. He raised the collar of his jacket closer to his ears, and ran after the twirling hat.

"Man, not again," murmured Frank under his breath.

His hat had blown off his head. Each time he reached down to get it, the wind blew it beyond his reach. It was as if the hat was toying with him. For the fourth time, it blew several yards out of his reach. Although he was late for work and had others hats, he wasn't about to give up. The hat didn't look like much after having been washed in the machine by an over-exuberant eleven year old, but it was Frank's prized possession.

Minutes later, practically out of breath, Frank found himself alone near the rear of the park in a remote area—a section he had never explored before. The hat had landed on a large weathered cardboard box beneath a huge weeping willow. The tree's branches fanned out like a beautiful green canopy that draped the ground beneath.

An eerie feeling washed over him as he surveyed the area. Due to much rain in the last month, the entire park was overgrown and in need of maintenance. Yet, in the midst was a patch about the size of a small vehicle of trampled grass. To his right, Frank noticed a rusted, shopping cart half-filled with crushed aluminum cans.

Suddenly, Frank sensed he wasn't alone, even before he noticed the run down dirty sneakers that extended from the box.

As quickly and as quietly as possible, he tiptoed within inches of the body and gently retrieved his hat. He dared not take his eyes off the box. He retreated as he gently tapped the hat on his leg and extracted tiny pieces of debris.

In an instant, the top of the box was hurled into the air. A small-framed, elderly woman sprang to her feet. Her piercing eyes were devoid of fear, and she advanced toward him. Her arms were slightly extended in a backward defense mode.

She wore an oversized, red wool coat with stained, gray baggy sweats. It looked as though she was wearing several layers. She wore a pilot-type hat with ear flaps that buttoned under her chin. Crowfeet circled her eyes and deep wrinkles creased across her forehead. She had a small crescent shaped scar or birthmark by her right eye. It was hard to tell her age. She looked to be in her sixties but moved with the agility of a much younger woman.

She eyed him suspiciously.

To calm her, Frank immediately threw his arms up in a surrendering manner. He was not sure what was happening.

"I'm sorry. I didn't mean to disturb you. I was....I was just getting my hat. The wind blew it over here," he added.

He wasn't sure she understood English. The dirt and neglect made it impossible to tell her nationality. She could easily be a tanned Caucasian, a bronzed Hispanic or a fair-skinned African- American. Regardless, Frank was moved with compassion.

How long had she been living here? Days? Weeks? Months? Where was her family? Why wasn't she in a shelter?

She turned her head sharply as faint singing could be heard in a distance. A look of panic appeared across her face. A distant voice singing, "I don't know why my baby left me," drew closer. Frank recognized the voice. It belonged to the ground caretakers. He sang the same song all the time. Frank had teased him on one occasion about constantly singing about why his baby left him. He replied that it didn't make sense to change his song until he learned the reason why she left.

"Git! GiT! She ordered between clenched teeth and with a wave of her hand as the caretaker's voice grew closer. Clearly, she was perturbed. Frank noticed a slight limp as she grabbed her belongings. She piled them on a cart, shoved it between bushes, and spread the branches over to conceal it.

Not wanting to draw attention to the woman nor wanting to be responsible for disclosing her hideout Frank rushed several yards away from the tree as the caretaker approached. He bent down and pretended to tie his shoe.

Dressed in khaki and a heavy plaid lumber jacket the caretaker greeted him as usual. "Good morning, V-i-e-t-n-a-m!" he sang. It was a line from one of his favorite movies. He jabbed his stick into a pop can and tossed it into the garbage cart he was pulling.

"Good morning," said Frank as he stood up.

"Mighty windy today," the caretaker announced.

"Yes, yes it is," Frank responded, looking up as the dark clouds rolled overhead.

"Gotta move on before the rain comes," he added, as he tipped his hat.

"Yes, yes, indeed."

Frank reached down and pretended to tie his other shoe as the caretaker hurriedly made his way down the path. Confident that the caretaker was out of hearing, Frank walked back to the tree only to find that the woman was gone and so was her cart.

She couldn't have gotten far, Frank thought. He turned around and around, as his eyes scanned the park. He felt something underneath his foot and stepped back to see an old coin purse with a broken clasp held together with a rubber band. He picked it up but hesitated to open it. Again, he scanned the park. There was no one in sight. He opened it in search of identification. Inside was a small locket with a picture of a woman holding a little girl with a big smile, two quarters and six one-dollar bills. No identification. Again, he scanned the park. He was alone.

A strong breeze blew against his back and the sky had darkened. He took off his hat to avoid a repeat occurrence. After all, this wasn't just a hat. This was a piece of Annette, a piece of his heart. She had given it to him on his 35th birthday. It was the last gift she'd given him.

As Frank made his way across the park he relived the day she had given it to him.

It had been the Saturday before Christmas. He had taken the family downtown to see the beautiful window decorations and the lighting of the city's Christmas tree. Annette and the girls had "ooohed" and "aaahed" at merchandise in each window. Frank and his son, Marcus, quietly trailed behind them mocking.

Then he saw the hat. Perched on a Clark Gable-looking mannequin was the coolest hat he'd ever seen. It was navy and maroon tweed with a narrow brim; a small feather jutted out from the side.

"Daddy," cried Lindsey, as she yanked on his sleeve. Annette looked back to see him staring at the hat. She smiled.

Daddy, can I have some hot chocolate?

"May I?" he corrected.

"May you what?" she asked innocently. Frank patiently explained the difference between using the phrases "May I?" and "Can I?"

"*Was I that bad?*" *asked Sheila.*

"*No, dear,*" *replied Annette but quickly added,* "*You were worse.*" *Sheila's haughty look quickly dissipated.*

"*Just kidding,*" *said Annette, pulling Sheila close.*

"*Anybody else wants hot chocolate?*" *Frank asked.*

"*No.*"

"*No. Not me.*"

"*I'll take a coffee with extra cream and sugar,*" *Marcus answered.*

"*Sure, son; sure,*" *Frank retorted.*

"*Honey, take Lindsey. We'll wait here,*" *Annette requested, as she glanced at the hat.*

"*Okay. Lindsey and I will be back in a jiffy with not one but two chocolate mustaches,*" *he teased as he grabbed Lindsey's hand.*

After Frank and Lindsey returned it was obvious that something secretive had transpired. Marcus smiled and fidgeted the entire evening. His perpetual smirk betrayed him. Frank knew his son was trying very hard to keep a secret. He was sure it was about a Christmas gift.

A drop of rain on the side of his face brought Frank out of his reverie. He looked up and noticed how quickly the sky had changed. As far as he could see, the sky was blanketed with charcoal gray mingled with deep streaks of black. An individual didn't have to be a meteorologist to know what that meant. He held onto his hat and cut across the park.

Chapter 2

A few yards away, confident that she was alone, the elderly woman stepped from behind the bushes, only yards from where Frank had stood. The cart was now filled with several large trash bags. She pulled a wide piece of plastic from her pocket, covered the cart and tucked the sides in to protect all of her worldly possessions.

With showers approaching, she pulled a long plastic poncho from her bags, slipped it over her head and made her way across the park. The heavens opened and the rain poured. In seconds there was practically zero visibility. She crossed the street cautiously.

To keep her cart in view, she propped it in front of the window at Joe's Diner. The overhead awning shielded her from the rain, as she peered inside the eatery. The diner was practically empty. A lone postal carrier sat at the counter texting. Relieved, she pulled the poncho over her head and shook it off. Soaking from the rain and shivering from the cold, she went inside.

The aroma of fresh perked coffee and baked bread made her stomach growl. She hadn't eaten since lunch the day before. A woman from a neighborhood shelter had invited her to come and eat daily. She had thanked her, but chose to pick up cans to provide for her sustenance.

The waitress smiled. "Good morning, Mrs. Pauley; the usual?"

Mrs. Pauley nodded and sat near the window to keep an eye on her cart. Some mischievous teenagers had once pushed it down the streets, into an alley. Although nothing was taken, the childish horseplay had caused her a lot of grief. A nice gentleman saw what happened and kindly returned the cart to her. She was determined to never let it out of her sight again. Everything she owned was in that cart. Everything that was dear to her. Well, almost everything.

She usually took her food back to the park and ate alone. The heavy rainfall, however, forced her to eat inside the diner. As Mrs. Pauley poured milk on her oatmeal, added a teaspoon of sugar, and a pat of butter, she smiled. This was the only way she could get her daughter Lisa to eat oatmeal when she was a child.

As the rain descended, Mrs. Pauley sat quietly. She stared out the window. She remembered happier times, and smiled.

When Lisa was two years old, Mrs. Pauley and Lisa's father, Albert, had taken her to the toy store. She was dressed in a cute, pink short outfit with matching ribbons in her hair. She was chatting away as usual. The clerk commented on how cute she looked. The clerk said, "You are such a cute doll."

Lisa shot back. "I'm not a dog; I'm a girl!"

The lady responded, "No, I said a doll."

Lisa relented, "Oh, I thought you said a 'woof, woof.'"

Mrs. Pauley's smile faded as she remembered her husband Albert.

They had met in high school when he was a senior and she a sophomore. He was struggling to pass English. After overhearing the librarian congratulate her on an English award she had received, he introduced himself and asked if she would tutor him. She was reluctant but agreed after many entreaties.

They studied on the porch several hours a week and found, to their surprise, that they had much in common. They enjoyed the same type of comedies and shared a fondness for pulling pranks.

The day of the final exam Albert was nervous but Pauley was confident that he was prepared.

A week after the exam, he called and said he was coming over. He sounded disheartened.

She felt sad. She had been so confident that he would do well on the exam. Maybe he had been too nervous because of past failures. He'd have to work harder for the next semester.

She tried valiantly to remember the words she would use to console him, as she met him on the porch. He thanked her for her help then added, "It is what it is." He pulled his rolled-up exam paper from his back pocket.

"I'm sorry."

He shrugged his shoulders.

She took a deep breath and unfolded the paper. Her mouth flew open, and she whacked him on the arm.

"Ouch; that hurts!"

"Good! That was mean," she laughed as she reviewed his paper.

A large A+ was scribbled across the top of the paper in red ink.

"Sorry. I'd like to make it up to you. Would you…like…like to go to the movies this weekend?

Lisa shook her head. "Sorry; but, no, I wouldn't."

He was crestfallen but tried not to show it. After all, he was a star athlete. He did not have an oversized ego but most of the girls at school would have been thrilled.

He forced a smile and thanked her. "I really appreciate all of your help. I couldn't have done it without you. I guess I'll see you around school."

He turned and walked off the porch.

"Albert, I wouldn't LIKE to go but I would LOVE to go to the movies with you," she teased.

He turned to see her hand at her folded lips, as she tried to suppress a laugh.

"Now that was mean; but it's okay. I admit; I had it coming."

She pulled on the door handle, "See you tomorrow."

He heard her giggle before she went into the house.

He giggled too.

Mrs. Pauley peered out of the window as pellets of rain continued to fall. She uttered, "Those were happy days."

"Did you say something, Mrs. Pauley?" asked the busboy, overhearing her mumble.

She shook her head.

"It's going to be a wet one," said the busboy as he cleared the tables.

"Yep," said the waitress halfheartedly as she sat at the counter and watched Mrs. Pauley. She wondered about her family. Did she have one? How did she end up on the street?

"Going to be a slow day," he added.

"Yep," the waitress agreed. She wondered if Mrs. Pauley had children.

"Today is my last day," he announced.

"Yes. What?"

"I was just teasing. Carol, you haven't heard a word I've said."

"Sorry. It's just…"

"I know. We all feel the same about Mrs. Pauley. She doesn't like to be asked questions so we don't. But, we can't help but wonder…"

"I know, I know," said Carol, and got up to greet a couple coming through the front door. They were drenched yet filled with laughter as they sat in a booth near Mrs. Pauley.

As Carol placed two glasses of water on their table Mrs. Pauley walked to the register. She frantically began to search her pockets. Her coin purse was missing. She rushed outside to check her cart.

Carol and the busboy watched as she searched the cart over and over. They knew she always kept her money in a beat up coin purse and were sure that was what she was searching for. They didn't know anything about Mrs. Pauley's life or family, but knew she wasn't a panhandler. She was fiercely independent and didn't take anything that wasn't hers. She didn't like freebies. They knew she wouldn't have peace accepting a free meal.

Finally, they saw she had given up the search. With a plan Carol went into action. She hurried over to where Mrs. Pauley had been sitting, took a five dollar bill out of her pocket, and placed it in the cushion of the seat. She busied herself at the counter as Mrs. Pauley came through the door.

"What's wrong? You lost something?" the waitress asked. Mrs. Pauley nodded.

"Well, let's look for it. What was it? Your money?"

Mrs. Pauley nodded again, as she followed Carol over to the booth. Carol pretended to look around as Mrs. Pauley again searched her pockets.

"It has to be here. Help me look," she encouraged Mrs. Pauley, wanting her to find the money.

Mrs. Pauley spotted the money, picked it up and gave it to her. "Oh, you found your money," Carol pretended.

Mrs. Pauley shook her head aggressively.

"Well, either way, this is yours. There is no way we can find out who lost it."

Mrs. Pauley shook her head a second time and thrust out her hand.

"Sorry, it's not mine," Carol responded. "Finder's keepers," she argued, as she walked to the register.

The couple was looking on and heard the entire conversation. The young lady spoke. "She's right you know. So many people come in here daily. There is no way to know whom the money belongs. So, it's yours."

The man agreed.

Mrs. Pauley turned and walked to the register. As she paid for her meal, Carol saluted. "Have a great day, Mrs. Pauley."

Mrs. Pauley smiled and nodded. After she turned from the register, her smile faded and was replaced by a look of sadness. The picture was gone. Her only picture of her daughter was gone. Brokenhearted, she walked out of the diner.

"I saw what you did," the busboy observed. "That was smooth, very smooth."

Carol gave a weak smile. She wished she could do more. There was a deep sadness about Mrs. Pauley.

"You know what?" asked the busboy.

Carol turned, "What?"

"You beat me to the punch," he waved a ten-dollar bill.

She smiled, "Great minds think alike."

The rain had stopped, and sunshine attempted to peek from underneath the clouds. Mrs. Pauley folded the poncho and pushed it down into the side of the cart. She hurried to hide her things in the park. It was getting late; she had to be downtown by noon. Dr. Ahmed was expecting her.

Chapter 3

A few miles away, Lisa lay in bed and stared at the ceiling. There was not a single day that she didn't think of her mother. Where was she? Was she okay? Did she miss her? Was she even ali....

She tried not to allow her thoughts to even go there.

Lisa threw back the comforter and crawled out of bed. There was a chill in the room. She grabbed her robe and tied it loosely. For the third night in a row she hadn't slept well. It had become a burden to go to a job that left her feeling drained and burdened down.

As she brushed her teeth, the rumbling sounds of thunder made her want to hop back in bed, pull the cover over her head and stay there. Unfortunately, today was not the day. Her supervisor had informed her two days earlier that she wasn't meeting her quota for the week. After an assessment, the supervisor had concluded that Lisa spent too much time listening to other people's problems. It was true that Lisa had spent too much time distracted by customers' complaints, but found it difficult to be blunt with them. Her listening seemed therapeutic for them. Lisa exhaled a sigh of despair as she rinsed off her toothbrush. She needed her job. Some way, she was going to have to figure out how to be firm yet gentle.

Lisa dreamed of one day becoming a librarian. She was drawn to books, maps, and references and loved helping people to explore and discover new and exciting things. For the past eight months, she'd inquired about openings each time she had visited the library. There were none. During this time Lisa had gotten to know the head librarian, who had once encouraged Lisa to send in a resume. There was a rumor that one of the librarians would be getting married soon and moving out of state. Lisa didn't hesitate. She hand delivered her resume, the next day.

As she brushed her hair in front of the dresser, Lisa challenged the lady in the mirror. "Today, be nice but firm. Remember your job is on the line. You don't have time for long sob stories."

Talking to a mirror was one thing but actually telling it to people was another, she thought, as she laid the brush down and finished dressing. She glanced at the clock. There was no time for breakfast. She pulled two bananas from the bunch, grabbed her purse, and umbrella, and hurried out the door.

*   *   *

As Lisa shook the rain off her umbrella in front of Joe's Diner, she was convinced the fruit could take the place of a warm bowl of oatmeal but, with only a few hours of sleep, there was no substitution for a hot cup of coffee.

"I'm so sorry," she apologized as she noticed her open umbrella had hit the back of a woman's head, caused her to lose her balance and stumble forward.

"Are you okay?" Lisa worriedly asked.

The woman nodded and hurried out onto the sidewalk. As Lisa sat in the booth, for the first time she saw the lady's face. As the woman fussed with a shopping cart, Lisa observed her from head to toe. There was something vaguely familiar about her. The woman wore a stained oversize red wool coat underneath a plastic rain poncho and rundown sneakers.

"Hi, my name is Carol. What can I get for you? A sunny day is not on the menu." She laughed at her own joke.

Lisa smiled. "That would be my first choice." She checked her watch and observed, "I'm sorry. I don't know why I sat down. I'm running late. Make it a coffee, extra cream and sugar to go, please."

"Alrightie then," Carol crowed as she folded her pad and stuck her pen behind her ear.

Chapter 4

"I understand, sir. Why I ….My hands are tied. Do you think you can make a partial payment today, Mr. Hall?" asked the voice on the other end of the line.

For the third time, Frank took a deep breath and repeated.

"Ma'am, I'm afraid I'm not able to do anything right now, nothing, absolutely nothing at all!"

He quickly added, "I hope to be able to catch up …." An aching feeling washed over his stomach as he shared a little about his situation and loss.

The representative claimed to understand his situation, yet went on to express that she was simply doing her job.

For the first few months after Annette's death, Frank found it more and more difficult to concentrate at work—that is, on the days when he went to work. His supervisor had covered for him as long as he could but eventually had to let him go. Frank wasn't surprised when he got his pink slip.

Frank didn't want to be rude but with nothing new to add to the conversation, he gently placed the phone on the nightstand. He picked the comforter off the floor and threw it onto the bed before he walked out of the room. He could hear the agent muffled voice repeat the conversation again, as though she was reading from a script.

As he walked into the bathroom Frank caught a glimpse of his reflection in the mirrored shower door. He'd lost weight that he couldn't afford to lose. The well-groomed man who took pride in his appearance, shaved every day and got his hair cut every two weeks was gone. A man with a lined face, bags beneath his eyes, and disheveled hair stared back at him. He raked tiny pieces of blue lint from his hair.

He took his razor from the medicine cabinet, untangled the cord and plugged it into the electrical outlet beneath the light switch. With the razor on his cheeks Frank stared into the mirror. The image testified to what he knew. He'd let himself go much too long, yet, he didn't often have enough energy to turn the switch on. He placed the razor back inside the medicine cabinet and walked down the stairs into the kitchen.

Loneliness rushed over Frank as he walked into the kitchen. It was not only where they always ate as a family (Annette opposed the children eating in from of the television or in their bedrooms) but the kitchen table was where they had family game night. Annette often bought two of the same puzzles from the dollar store and they would compete to see who'd finish first. The loser would have to fix the snacks for their movie night.

Also, all homework was done at the kitchen table to eliminate the back and forth, up and down the stairs when the kids had questions. It was also where the monthly budget and weekly menu were discussed. It was the hub of the house.

A year had passed since Annette's death. Unlike what many had told him, the passage of time had not made her loss any easier to handle.

Frank sat down but his eyes were glued to the empty chair at the other end of the table.

"Good morning, Daddy," sang Lindsey, as she turned from the fridge, wrapped her arms around his neck and gave him a big hug.

"Morning, baby," Frank replied as he playfully twisted her nose and tucked one of her long braids behind her ear. Lindsey, five, was in kindergarten. He was relieved that she was adjusting to Annette's absence so well.

"Good morning, kids," Frank chimed as he picked up the morning paper.

Sheila, eleven, his middle daughter, slowly waved her hand and hurriedly ate her cereal.

She was beginning to become interested in boys and cared about her appearance. Annette would be pleased to know that Sheila took pride in her appearance.

Angie looked up and waved. She was thirteen, his oldest child. An avid reader who loved sports, her head was bowed over in a book as her fingers fished slices of grapefruit from a bowl. Frank cleared his throat as nine year old Marcus, oblivious to what was going on, played on a game he held in his hand.

Frank cleared his throat again.

"Sorry, sorry, Dad," Marcus apologized. "Ah, good morning," he added.

Angie looked up from her reading and spoke. "Hi, Dad," Angie spoke. She quickly remembered and laid her book aside. "Sorry, I was just looking at one last thing."

Annette had always stressed that meal time was family time to enjoy each other's company. No television, radio, telephone or books were allowed at the table during meals.

While Sheila ate her breakfast, Frank had noticed that her lips were bright pink.

"Wow," cried Marcus noticing them for the first time.

Sensing eyes on her, Sheila looked up and asked, "What?"

Frank gave her a look that answered, "You know what."

Sheila bellowed, "This isn't lipstick. It is lip gloss. What? My lips are chapped."

"You know what's good for chapped lips….," Frank began.

Sheila interrupted him. "I know, I know; use Vaseline." She said as she wiped the lip gloss off with a paper napkin and left the room.

"Thanks, honey," Frank directed toward her.

No response.

"Dad, when can I wear lipstick?" asked Lindsey.

"When you are old enough to get a job…"

"I have a job," finished Lindsey. "I help Mrs. Green rake leaves."

"When you are old enough for a real job," Frank countered.

"Oh, you mean when I'm a teenager?"

"Affirmative," Angie interjected, as she stacked her books and pushed her chair from the table. She walked over to the sink, rinsed her glass and filled it with water.

"Dad, make her stop using those big words," Lindsey begged.

"I can't do that, honey. She's learning new words by using them."

Lindsey's sad face prompted him to ad lib, "I tell you what. Every time she uses a big word, she has to tell you what it means. That way you'll learn along with her. Is it a deal?"

"Deal," Lindsey rejoined.

She rolled her eyes, folded her lips and thought for a moment. She got up and walked over to the sink near Angie.

"What does A-farm-and-a-T mean?" Lindsey asked.

"No, it's affirmative," corrected Angie before she gulped down the glass of water.

"That's what I said," Lindsey shot back.

"No, you… ah, forget it. Affirmative means to agree," she explained before wiping water from her mouth with the back of her hand.

"Well, why you didn't just say, 'I agree,'" asked Lindsey throwing up her hands as Angie made her lunch.

"Daddy, did you see the sticker Ms. Shannon gave me today?" she asked as she held up a shiny red heart about the size of her hand.

"You mean, yesterday" corrected Frank.

"Yes, I mean, yesterday; I got it mixed up. Did you see it?"

"No, I didn't honey," he acknowledged. He folded his paper and waited with anticipation.

Lindsey walked over to him with an outstretched hand. She smiled from ear to ear as she displayed it.

"See," she intoned, "Ms. Shannon, she gave me this as a show of kindness; I helped Dee Dee clean up the milk she spilled. It was all over the floor, all everywhere!"

While Frank was busy with Lindsey Marcus picked up his game and began playing again.

"You mean Ms. Shannon gave it…"

"That's what I said; Ms. Shannon, she gave me the heart," Lindsey added.

"No, not Ms. Shannon, she," he tried to explain.

"Dad, she doesn't get it like you and I," reminded Angie.

"I do get it. It is right here," she insisted as she held up the heart.

Angie gave her father a look that said, "I rest my case."

Frank smiled and gave Lindsey a big hug. He quietly waved Angie out of the room.

"Don't forget your umbrella," Frank reminded them as he looked out the kitchen window. "The rain has stopped for now but it is supposed to start again this afternoon."

"Okay!" they chorused. Frank turned to find Marcus clicking away on his game.

He cleared his throat extremely loud. Marcus looked up to an empty table.

"Where is everybody?" he asked absentmindedly.

Frank stared as he patted his foot and calmly took a deep breath.

"Oh, I think I know." Marcus deadpanned.

"Good bye, Dad."

"Good bye, son; have a great day."

"And, son."

"Yeah, Dad?"

"Leave the game on the table."

Chapter 5

"Mr. Hall?"

No response, then, the sound of the dial tone. Emotionally drained, Lisa hung the phone up. Clearly, she wasn't cut out for this line of work. It broke her heart hearing the despair in the voice of many of the callers. Sickness, death, divorce and, yes, sometime overspending cause many to have their vehicles repossessed. Some had just three or four payments left. She shook her hands in a futile attempt to shake off a feeling of heaviness. Hopefully, she'd get the job at the library.

She looked at the file again. Something about this caller, a Frank Hall, had moved her. Most of the time the men talked tough but there was a despondency in the caller's voice. She tried to literally shake it off. She knew that stress and depression were detrimental to physical health.

Lisa pulled her purse from the bottom drawer, opened her billfold and pulled her mom's picture out. She fought back tears. She identified with this caller. Even though it had been years since she last saw her mom, it was still painful because she didn't have closure. Hearing her supervisor's footsteps, she finished off the second banana and drank the last of her cold coffee. She tossed the cup and peel into the wastebasket. She put her picture and purse into the drawer and reached for the next file. Rain from the umbrella had formed a puddle under her desk, which reminded her of the homeless looking woman at the diner.

Chapter 6

The sound of the neighbor's dog jarred Frank back to the present. He looked up from the table, and was surprised to find himself alone. Had he said good-bye to the children before they left for school? He was beginning to get worried. On several occasions in the last few weeks there were periods of time he couldn't recall.

"I got to get a grip," he whispered as he laid his head on the table. His kids needed him more than ever. He would have to pull himself together; for their sake, at least, if not his own.

"Rinnnggggggggggg."

"No, please, not another bill collector." After the fourth ring, he walked over to the phone, checked the caller ID, and walked up the stairs.

Frank stared into the small walk-in closet he had shared with Annette. Everything on her side was neat and orderly, organized according to seasons and colors. Her sweaters and sweat pants were on the bottom shelf.

Frank knew that he had to pack her things and give them away. He couldn't keep putting it off forever; maybe tomorrow, but definitely not today.

After the funeral Helen, Annette's best friend since high school, had promised to help him pack and give away her things. There were several ladies in the family that could use and would love them. A year had passed; nonetheless, he wasn't able to emotionally do it, not just yet. He slowly closed the door.

He walked around the room with mixed emotions. Everything in it reminded him of her. A part of him wanted to keep things just as they were but deep down he knew he needed some sort of closure. For the children sake he needed to move on. Annette would want him to go on with his life.

He longed for her embrace. He took her robe off the back of the closet door and wrapped it around himself. He rubbed its velour against his face and inhaled her cologne. The scent of the familiar smell aroused memories of her presence, but the limp robe crystallized her absence.

Through the partially opened window came the sound of a soft hum from the neighbor's central air unit. The white crisp curtains swayed back and forth as a cool breeze filled the room, bringing with it a heavy smell of Gardenias. The glossy green foliage was beautiful even when they hadn't bloomed. All summer, Annette had cut and placed them in vases throughout the house.

Frank managed a weak smile as he remembered the day they'd planted them.

Annette had researched plants at the library earlier that week and had decided on begonias and impatiens. Her research completed, Annette had planned to pick up the flowers at a small roadside nursery out in the country and plant them early on a Saturday morning while the dew was still on the ground.

Friday during lunch hour, Frank shared with the supply clerk his plan for the weekend.

She encouraged him to plant some gardenias. He hadn't planned to do any actual planting, only to till the soil. But after the clerk pulled up a picture of gardenias on his phone, Frank nodded in agreement. He knew Annette would love them. They reminded Frank of roses, and Annette loved roses. He also learned roses symbolized love and romance and they complimented begonias. He was confident of his decision.

They picked the necessary supplies from the hardware store: a hoe, fertilizer and bags of topsoil. They were excited about becoming "city gardeners" as Grandma Kate had characterized them when they shared their plan. She was born in the South, still had dirt under her fingernails from her life on the farm. She said she wasn't about to add any more.

With the windows down, the cool breeze felt great as Frank and Annette drove into the country. They listened to Diana Ross's sultry voice on the radio and enjoyed the solitude they shared. They reached the nursery just before it closed. The clerk helped them select gardenias, impatiens, and some other annuals and perennials. She answered all of their questions, offered additional suggestions and tips, and gave them a store discount. They were delighted.

They decided to stop at a 24-hr truck stop where breakfast was served around the clock. Crispy slab bacon; mouthwatering thin buttermilk pancakes with maple syrup; fluffy, soft scrambled eggs; and fresh, perked coffee rounded off a perfect evening... until the ride home.

A white Ford Explorer with a hanging side mirror and Indiana license plates cut in front of them, which nearly caused an accident. Frank was furious and chased after the driver of the truck. For over a mile Annette pleaded with him to stop the chase but to no avail. Annette was in a panic. Desperate, she faked an emergency. She held her mouth, inflated her jaws and motioned for Frank to pull over. He did. She got out and started walking along the Interstate. Frank was confused. He caught up with her and asked "What's wrong?"

"What's wrong? What's wrong? Are you kidding me?"

She looked incredulous at him.

He looked clueless at her.

"Do you realize how fast you were going? And if you had caught up with the truck, then what?" she asked.

He said nothing. She turned and continued to walk along the shoulder of the Interstate.

He caught up with her again and pleaded for her to get back in the car.

"Frank, I am not going to ride with someone who doesn't value his life. If you do not value your own you cannot possibly value mine."

After much persuasion, and a promise to never do it again, she returned to the truck.

That night was a typical warm spring one, yet, there was a chill in their home. It was no different that Saturday morning during breakfast. They were both quiet: Annette because of disappointment and Frank because of guilt. To break the silence Frank turned on the television.

Local television stations were reporting that a robbery had occurred at a roadside market less than a mile from the nursery. The getaway vehicle was a white Ford Explorer with a hanging side mirror and Indiana license plates. The driver believed to be armed and dangerous was still at large. The timeline put Frank and Annette in the area at the time of the robbery.

Annette didn't say a word. She didn't have to. Frank had chills from the thought of what could have happened. He reached for her hand. As he held it, he said "I'm sorry." She looked deep into his eyes and said "I know."

It had been fifteen years since they said "I do."

Now, it had been a year since…

"Baby, how I miss you," he cried.

With a sinking feeling in the pit of his stomach, he sat on the side of the bed. Each day was getting harder. He wanted to cry but was afraid that if he allowed himself to shed a tear, even one, that he wouldn't be able to control himself.

"Annette. Oh, how I miss you, honey."

He smiled when he remembered how she would always say, "I'm your bestiest friend and don't you ever forget it" right before she had to give him constructive criticism. It never fail, it made whatever she had to say easier to accept.

Frank stood in the middle of the floor and just looked around the room. Everything in the room reminded him of moments with her. Although the room was small, only about 10 by 15 square feet, it looked much larger. Annette had filled the wall opposite the window with mirrors, which gave the room the illusion of a much larger room. She had put much time and energy into making it the perfect little place to relax. She had teased him, saying it had to be special like a castle, since it was obvious that her man was a "king." After all, who else would a "queen" be married to? She had painted the room white and put up a blue border. Not being able to find the pictures she wanted she had taken scraps from the border and framed them for the walls.

Further, she had placed blue shag rugs at the foot and on each side of the bed. The comforter was white with blue stripes. He knew she had wanted the one with pink roses, but she had insisted on getting one that wasn't too "girlie"; after all, it was their room not just hers.

Oh, how he missed her.

He walked over to the dresser. Everything was pretty much like she had left it. He wanted to hold on to that feeling even though he knew she wouldn't be coming home again. Her comb and brush lay on top of a hand mirror with her daily planner and two decks of unopened cards. Frank smiled. Annette had learned how to play Bid Whiz from her grandmother and she loved it. She didn't play for money- which was a good thing- she was very competitive. Many of her friends refused to be her partner. They argued that she took the game too seriously. In defense, she always quoted her grandmother, "Life is like a Whiz game. You have to have strategies but, at the end of the day, it comes down to simply playing the hand you have been dealt."

Frank pulled open the bottom drawer. From underneath her underwear, he removed a small treasure box where Annette had kept her prized possessions; gold earrings and a charm bracelet her grandmother had given her. She had planned to give them to Angie as a graduation gift. Frank took out her wedding band. After the funeral, he had placed it in the box. He sat the box on the dresser as he held the ring tight in his clenched hand. With his eyes closed, he relived the day he had placed it on her finger with the promise to replace it as soon as he graduated from college and got a better paying job.

Unfortunately, three months after their wedding, Annette became pregnant. Frank had to discontinue college to provide for his family.

Would his heart ever stop hurting? Would he ever stop missing his wife? He wasn't even sure he wanted to. He placed the band back in the box, tucked it underneath her underwears and closed the drawer.

Twelve months....twelve long months. Yet, in a way, it felt like yesterday when he'd gotten the call that would forever change his life.

It had been an unusually warm Friday morning in late March. Frank had worked the overnight shift and had eaten breakfast with the kids before they left for school. Usually the kids walked to school but Annette had dropped them off on her way to the grocer. Less than an hour later, Marsha, a neighbor and store clerk, had called Frank and asked him to meet her at the hospital. Two hours later...just like that...Annette was gone...An aneurism.

If only he could have held her one more time. Told her how much he loved her one more time. If only...

Chapter 7

Frank recognized Angie's voice coming from outside of his window. He slowly rose from the chair and walked across the room. His heart was heavy. Had he made the right decision? Had he overreacted? After the discussion with Angie, it dawned on him that it would be difficult to raise four children, alone. Annette, somehow, always managed to make it seem easy.

Earlier in the day, he had made Angie change twice out of her sister's clothes. Sheila was two years younger and inches shorter.

He pulled back the curtains and noticed that they were dusty and in need of a washing. Like many other things, he placed their cleaning on his "to do" list.

"You should have known what your dad was going to say? Why did you ask him how it looked, anyway?" Angie's best friend Shanta asked.

"Because…," Angie's voice trailed off.

"Because what? You knew he was going to say it was too short. You knew he was going to say you couldn't wear it." Shanta accused.

"My mom used to ….but now; well, he's my dad! Now, let's go! This subject is closed."

"Your dad is so old fashioned," Shanta convicted without due process.

"What do you expect? He'll be 36 in October. Now, let's go. I have to be home by 8:00."

"8:00?"

"Yes, 8:00! Let's go!" Angie stormed off the porch. Shanta looked perplexed at her, threw her hands in the air, and hurried to catch up.

Frank smiled at the way Angie had handled the situation. A month earlier Shanta had talked Angie into cutting an English class when their teacher was absent. In the last few months Frank had noticed a big change in his oldest daughter. She had become more of a leader and less of a follower. Annette would have been proud.

Oh, how he missed his wife, his best friend. He missed the way she would snuggle close behind him in bed and wrap her (always cold) feet around his legs. She laughed at his jokes no matter how many times she had heard them. He missed the way she would softly stroke the back of his neck while they watched television. Gone was the smell of her soft-scented cologne.

He walked over to the dresser and picked up the cologne. After holding it to his chest for a moment he slowly squirted a tiny sweet-scented mist into the air. Frank smiled as he held the bottle close to his chest and remembered the last time they had gone out to dinner. It had been her parents' 38th wedding anniversary.

As usual Frank dressed first. He waited patiently as Annette walked back and forth from the bathroom, chatting on and on about something. He couldn't remember what. As she reached for her cologne, he spontaneously grabbed it from her hand, squirted gently on her wrists, and clasped her hands behind his neck.

"Annie, I know today is not our anniversary but I just want you to know I'm so glad you are my wife. These fifteen years have truly been the best years of my life. I have a terrific wife, a great son, and three beautiful daughters. Hands down, I'm the happiest man on planet Earth."

"Now look," she placed her fingers on his lips, "Don't make me cry. It took thirty minutes to fix this face. You are not going to have me looking like an owl before we leave the house."

He had taken her hands and softly kissed each of them. "I look forward to celebrating our 38th, 48th, 58th and even more with you."

Frank's heart ached. He choked back tears as he placed the bottle back on the dresser. Without a warning, he did something that he hadn't done since her death. He broke down and cried. First, it was a soft sob. Within seconds, he had slumped in the chair and cried uncontrollably.

"Dad, Dad, are you okay?" came a worried small voice from the hall. It was Lindsey.

"Daddy's okay," he replied, trying to sound composed. He took a deep breath and tried to pull himself together. He knew what Lindsey's next question would be:

"Dad, can I see?"

"Yes, you can" He quickly drew the blinds and hoped she wouldn't see the redness of his eyes. Lindsey pushed open the door and stood in the doorway scanning the room.

"It's dark in here," Lindsey observed and reached for the light switch.

"Let it stay off, baby; Daddy just want to sit for a moment."

"Dad, you thinking about mommy?" she asked as she stood in the doorway.

"Yes," he admitted with a lump in his throat.

In a flash she flew across the room and climbed up on his lap. She gave him a big hug.

She felt the dampness of his cheeks and assured him, "We are going to take care of you, daddy." It took every ounce of his strength not to fall apart.

"Thanks, Lindsey. We are going to take good care of each other." He smiled and tickled her nose.

"Dad?"

"Huh?"

"I miss mom but I'm happy I still have you. There is a boy in my room at school named Johnny; he cries all the time. Some of the boys were being mean to him, calling him a baby; but I was his friend. Miss Mason told us he lost his dad. Now everybody plays with him, so he won't be too sad, but he still cries sometime."

Frank hugged his daughter close.

"Dad, can Johnny stay with us and you can be his dad, too? Then he'll be happy just like me."

"What about his mom and the rest of his family? I'm sure they love him as much as I love you? You know what he needs? Friends. He needs good friends."

"Ah, Daddy, he has a lot of friends now. He has our whole class and Miss Mason."

"He'll be fine. Hey, let's make some tacos for lunch."

"Yea," shouted Lindsey as she ran ahead of him.

As he walked into the kitchen, Frank cleared his throat loudly as Lindsey opened the fridge.

"Sorry, I forgot. Rule one: wash up, first."

They both washed at the kitchen sink.

"Dad, I like cooking with you."

"I like cooking with you, too, honey." Frank opened the fridge and passed her the head of lettuce. Lindsey hummed as she washed and broke the lettuce into small pieces. Frank smiled. Annette always hummed while she cooked. Unlike most of the women in the family Annette enjoyed cooking.

"You are my sous chief".

"Sushi?"

"No, sous chef. That's the person who's second in charge to the chef," he explained.

"Aahh!"

She glowed with delight as she cut up a small bowl of cherry tomatoes with a butter knife.

It was less work to make the tacos himself, Frank thought, as he looked at the tomato juice on the counter and lettuce on the floor; however, it wasn't nearly as much fun. Frank smiled and reached for a paper towel.

*   *   *

"Great tacos, Dad," Marcus stated as he tilted his head back and devoured another piece.

"You can cook just like mom," he added before reaching for another shell.

Frank smiled. "Save some for your sisters."

Only a growing boy with a voracious appetite would compare a meal consisting of tacos and a garden salad to one of Annette's. Her father had been head chef in one of the best steak houses in the city for more than 20 years. As a teenager, Annette, very much "a daddy's girl," had often worked in the restaurant during the summer. She'd become a great cook.

She didn't believe "special" dinners were for holidays. Her philosophy was "everyday was a special day when you are blessed to share it with family and friends." She went to great pain to create each of her meals. It wasn't unusual for Frank and the kids to be awaken by the smell of homemade cinnamon rolls or French toast. Lasagna or chicken and dressing were just a request away. And to Frank's amazement, she did it on a budget of clipping coupons and centering her menu on what was in season or on sale.

"Dad, you could be cooking on television like that Bam, Bam, man," Lindsey encouraged him as she piled the cheese and lettuce high on her shell.

"Thanks, honey," he smiled feeling pretty good. But before he could savor the moment, someone threw a dart at his bubble.

"Yeah! Great meal; just like mom's," Sheila smirked, as she piled shredded cheese on her taco.

Frank asked, "Would you like to make dinner tomorrow and show us your culinary skills?"

"Ah, on second thought, "she cleared her throat, "great meal, Dad."

*   *   *

Frank looked up as he heard the key in the lock.

"Back already? I wasn't expecting you so soon," he said while noticing the clock. It was 7:55.

Angie gave a weak grin. She perceived the satire.

"Come on, Dad; the mall was crowded and the buses were slow."

"So, what did you get?" he asked anxious to see how she faired. This was the first time she'd gone shopping without adult supervision.

She proudly opened the bag and took out a large shoe box.

"How much did they cost?" he asked, eyeing the brand name logo. "A $150.00," she answered proudly, remembering that the cashier said she'd saved $60.

"What? $150.00?"

"Yes, but they are not just ordinary boots. These are snakeskin by..."

"I don't care who they are by. They are going back to the store."

He reached into the box and held up both boots. "For $150, you should have gotten the whole snake."

Lindsey snickered. Angie shot her a threatening look, which prompted her to hide behind her dad. Lindsey peeped out at her sister and licked out her tongue.

"But, Dad," wailed Angie, ignoring her little sister.

"Sorry, honey, but they go back first thing in the morning. I gave you $300 for boots, sneakers, and a couple of outfits."

"Well, I thought I could buy what I wanted.'

"No!"

He continued. "Look, I'm sorry. My name is not Bill Gates; neither is it Michael Jordan. I don't have money like that."

Lindsey asked, "Dad, are you broke?"

Well, let's put it this way—I'm closer to being broke than I am to being rich."

"Huh?" asked Lindsey looking confused.

"Lindsey, please!"

"But, Dad…" pleaded Angie.

"What else did you get?" he asked as he noticed another bag.

She reluctantly opened the bag and pulled out a pair of designer's jeans and a jersey.

"How much do you have left?" he asked. She shrugged her shoulders.

"I got something to eat and bus fare."

"Well, how much?" he insisted.

"I owe Shanta $30," she said slightly above a whisper

He shook his head. "How much were the jeans?"

Silence.

"How much were the jeans, Angie? His voice rose.

"The jersey was $65 and the jeans were $65."

"Wow! You paid $65?" Lindsey bellowed. She turned to her dad, pulled on his sleeve and asked, "How much is $65?"

"Run your bathwater and start getting ready for bed, Lindsey. It's almost 8:30."

"8:30, that's all? Melissa and Carla can stay up 'til 11:00," she told her dad "and they are the same age as me. Why can't I stay up to 11:00?" she asked.

He gave her a look that required no words. Lindsey forced a big grin. "I'm just playing," she demurred.

Lindsey knew her sister well. She walked slowly toward the door and expected a reaction from Angie as she passed. Sure enough, Angie reached out to grab her.

"Dad!" Lindsey cried out in laughter, as she stuck her fingers in her ears and licked out her tongue once she was safely in the hallway.

"Lindsey!" her dad called out.

The sound of the pitter patter from Lindsey's feet could be heard as she ran up the stairs.

"Honey, don't get caught up in designers' clothes. Don't buy something because of a name. Your name is as good as any. If all you wanted is a name on your jeans, give me a marker I can do that for free".

She was very disappointed.

"Honey, don't get sucked into that kind of thinking. Clothes don't make you; not even designer clothes. If you are a lazy student who wears resale clothes and makes F's in school, you'll be a lazy student who wear designers' clothes and makes F's in school. The only difference is that you will have saved a lot of money wearing the resale clothes."

"Honey, come sit down."

Angie took a deep breath and walked over to the couch. She prepared herself for a lecture.

"Let me share something with you that your mom told me years ago. One young lady she worked with bragged that she wouldn't be caught dead wearing resale clothes. Everybody knew it. One day the young lady bought a $400 suit from a fancy, downtown boutique. The sale's clerk had knocked off $50 because one of the buttons was missing from a sleeve and a tiny stain on the collar. The young lady brought pictures to work and was showing everybody at lunch. Turned out one of the other ladies on the job had worn the suit to a wedding and returned it to the same store minus … you guessed it, minus one button and a tiny stain on the collar. Honey, practically everything you buy out of a store has been tried on by many people so it's already used."

"But, Dad, you don't understand."

"Yes, I do. I was once a teenager. I admit it was a l-o-n-g time ago."

Angie smiled.

"Honey, I wish we could afford it but we can't. First thing in the morning I want you to take them back." His tone was non-negotiable. She nodded and walked out of the room with her head down.

Chapter 8

The alarm sounded. Lisa reached for the clock but knocked it to the floor. She turned it off and placed it on the nightstand. It was 6:30 a.m. As she yawned and stretched, she remembered her dream.

The setting was a beautiful banquet hall. It was her wedding day. She stood by a huge bay window. The ceiling was high with teardrop chandeliers. The room was filled with lots of people seated at long tables. The rose centerpieces on each table permeated the room. She wore a simple white chiffon dress. A hand touched her shoulder. It was her mom.

Lisa always dreamed. She remembered the details sometimes; sometimes she did not. Sometimes the dreams made sense to her; other times they didn't. She typically brushed them off, but this dream resonated with her. Was it a sign or just wishful thinking?

At 7:10, Lisa headed for the shower. As she brushed her teeth afterward, she recalled her past dating experiences. She'd dated only a couple of guys but one left an indelible impression. Lisa shivered as she remembered the event.

His name was Ronald, and they often rode the same train to work. They were both late for work one Friday and literally ran into each other as they climbed the stairs to the train platform. Lisa often caught him watching her while she read the paper, though she pretended not to notice. About a month after their collision he asked her out on a date; she agreed, however, she didn't feel comfortable enough to give him her address. Since he didn't own a car, it was a moot point. They agreed to meet at the movies and have dinner at an adjacent restaurant.

Lisa loved romance movies, but, a romance on the first date was definitely not an option.

They agreed on a Stephen King thriller, which had both of them shaking on the end of their seats. Lisa jumped into his arm several times. She would wonder later if his selection of a scary movie had been deliberate. Afterward, over dinner, they realized they had a lot in common; they talked about everything from sports to space travel.

Since it was their first date, Lisa insisted on paying for her meal. Surprisingly, he didn't object.

It was a warm Friday evening in late October. The Indian summer brought out a crowd of revelers who wanted to bask in the pleasant days before winter arrived.

They discussed the movie as they strolled down the street. A young mother pushed a stroller toward them, and Lisa walked around the pole to avoid the stroller. Ronald stepped back and also walked around the pole.

When Lisa walked around another pole, Ronald asked her not to split the pole. Lisa was confounded. He explained that it was bad luck to split a pole. Lisa laughed, thinking he was teasing. Then she saw the rage in his face. She knew he wasn't. She agreed not to split the pole. However, after that date, she made one last split. It was from him.

Lisa hummed as she got ready for work. Something about her mom being in her dream comforted her- even though she hadn't seen her mom in years.

Chapter 9

"Marcus!"

"Sorry, dad," Marcus apologized, as he pulled the milk carton from his lips. He wiped his mouth with the back of his hand and put the carton back in the fridge.

"Your last warning, son," Frank sneered. "Girls, remind me to pick up some milk tomorrow. Son, you can have the rest of that."

Embarrassed Marcus cleared his throat. "Dad, did you ever drink out of the carton when you were a kid?"

Frank wanted to say, "This isn't about me. This is about you." Yet, something about the girls' expression told him to proceed with caution.

"What are glasses for? Haven't you been taught to use a glass?" he asked, trying to avoid having to directly answer the question.

"Yes. Yes, I have, but Dad, did you?" Marcus pressed forward. Frank could recall Annette saying, "Lies come back to bite you in the butt."

He swallowed the lump in his throat. "Yes, I did son and I also paid the price for it." Unnerved by his son's persistence, Frank did not want the third degree and he had forgotten why he had come into the kitchen. He turned and headed back up stairs but not before he heard Sheila ask, "Why didn't you tell him what Mr. Jerome said about the juice?"

Jerome was Frank's best friend. They had known each other since fifth grade and had often spent the night at each other's house. Jerome told Marcus that one day after school he made a joke while Frank stood at the sink drinking grape juice out of the carton. Grape juice shot out of Frank's nose and splattered on the brand new white kitchen curtains.

"I wanted to see if he was going to tell the truth or?" said Marcus.

"Or what?" asked Lindsey.

"Or lie," whispered Sheila.

"Daddies and mommies don't lie," Lindsey objected.

"Sometimes they do," corrected Angie.

"I'm going to ask daddy," Lindsey shook.

"No," they shouted in unison.

Chapter 10

It was the last Monday in May, finally, the weather was getting warmer. While they watched the parade on television, Lindsey suggested a picnic in the park. Her siblings agreed and volunteered to fix the lunch.

After hours of volleyball, skating, swinging, Frank announced it was time to go home. With the food and drinks consumed, no one objected.

As they approached the entrance of the park, Marcus spotted an elderly man dressed in a military jacket and hollered out "Hey, mister!"

The elderly man looked up. Marcus saluted. The man countenance changed immediately.

"Dad, can we go and say hi to him?" Lindsey entreated.

Frank smile approvingly, "Of course." Lindsey hurried off as the whole family trailed behind her.

"Did you serve in the war? Do you have any medals?' inquired Lindsey.

"Did you ever get shot?" asked Marcus.

The vet was eager to share his story. He was a WW2 vet who had received a Silver Star for his bravery at Pearl Harbor on Dec. 7, 1941. He vehemently stated that he was no hero. He was a soldier defending his country.

The children were excited and listen with enthusiasm. He answered their many questions, some in great details, others, he brushed aside. Understandably, there was a lot he avoided sharing with the children.

After an hour, reluctantly, they had to say goodbyes.

As they pilled into the car, Frank noticed the vet had an audience. He stood surrounded by young boys, pointing to the insignias on his jacket, one by one.

Frank smiled. For the first time, he felt as though they had truly celebrated Memorial Day.

*   *   *

That night, Angie sat on the side of the bed and braided Sheila's hair. Lindsey was sprawled out in the floor, watching television.

"Are we going to stay with Grandma Kate?" asked Sheila.

"No, why?" asked Angie.

No reason; I was just wondering," shrugged Sheila.

A silence fell on the room.

Lindsey who usually tuned everything out when cartoons were on sat up straight and waited to hear more.

There was silence.

"Sheila, daddy is not going to send us to live with grandma and granddad, is he?" Lindsey asked. "I like spending the night with them but I want to stay here with daddy."

"No, Lindsey," Angie assured her.

"I know sometimes daddies...ouch! What did you do that for?" Sheila grabbed her head and turned in the chair to stare at Angie.

"Sorry," Angie apologized.

"I miss mom," Lindsey confided.

Angie rolled her eyes at Sheila, laid the comb on the bed and sat on the floor beside Lindsey.

"What I do?" asked Sheila as she held her head.

"I know; we all do. Dad misses mom, too. No, we do not have to stay with grandma and grandpa" Angie promised and looked at Sheila with a "don't say anything" expression in her eyes.

"Hey, hey, what's all the yelling about?" Frank bellowed. He'd been awakened out of a sound sleep. He turned over and picked up the alarm clock. It was 10:17. He slipped on his house shoes, and reached for his robe. As he walked across the hall he could hear the girls scrambling for bed.

"Do you girls realize what time it is?"

Lindsey sat up and announced proudly, "It's 10:18."

"And what time is your bed time, ladies?"

Lindsey answered with a question. "Why do we have to go to bed early? Melissa and Carla can stay up as long as she wants to, and she's five just like me."

"So you want to stay up as long as you want to, just like Melissa?" he queried. The older girls knew it was a loaded question. Neither answered.

Lindsey spoke with an air of rectitude, "Yes, we do."

"Okay," Frank replied. Lindsey was puzzled; she hadn't expected her dad to agree.

Frank walked over to the closet and opened the door. He pulled Lindsey's Hello Kitty tote from the shelf. He laid it on the bed beside her.

"Pack your stuff. I'll call Melissa's father and tell him you are coming to stay with them."

"No, I want to stay with you."

He bent down and kissed her on the forehead. "Staying with me means following my rules. Your mom and I agreed that 9:00 is late enough for you all to be up; it's non-negotiable. I know some children stay up all night but they shouldn't. You need a good night sleep. Do you understand?"

She nodded in agreement and crawled into bed. He tucked the sheet around her shoulder and smiled. Angie and Sheila also went back to bed.

"Good night, girls." Frank turned off the light. He made his way down stairs. He gulped down a glass of water and noticed through the window, a full moon. He closed the curtains. It brought back so many memories. He and Annette had often sat on the screened back porch on nights like this one.

He could hear Angie and Sheila bickering. He placed the glass in the sink and headed upstairs.

"Okay; what's the problem?" He asked, as he tapped on the door. No one said a word. He pushed the door open and turned on the light.

"Well!"

Angie and Sheila exchanged looks; neither said a word.

"Well!" he asked louder.

"I know," said Lindsey sitting up.

"L-i-n-d-s-e-y!"

Lindsey quickly pulled the sheet over her head. "Sorry," she mumbled under the cover.

"For the last time, what's the problem?"

Sheila hesitated. She didn't want to tell. "Angie got caught cheating on a math test today."

"Angie, is this true? I thought math was your favorite subject. What happened?"

Angie shrugged her shoulders and looked down at the floor. With rollers in her hair, she looked so much like her mom.

Frank knew it wasn't just him. Annette's death had taken a toll on the children as well. They tried not to show it but they were missing their mom. He could see it in their eyes, at the dinner table or when they walked into his bedroom.

Annette was so good with situations like these. She would always tell a story or something to help the children understand.

Lindsey scooted back near the wall as Frank sat down. He patted the bed for Angie to sit. She shrugged her shoulders, walked over and sat down next to her father.

He wondered how to handle the situation. However, before he could organize his thoughts, Angie blurted out, "It was just a test, a dumb test. No big deal." Her emotional outburst startled Frank, yet he should have known that his children quiet façade masked deep hurt.

Lindsey started wheezing lightly. Sheila jumped out of bed and grabbed Lindsey's pump. In seconds the asthma was under control. Lindsey breathed easily.

"Thank you, Sheila," sang Lindsey as she pulled the cover up around her neck.

"You're welcome, little sister," replied Sheila and climbed back in bed. She pulled the cover around her neck and waited to see how Angie was going to get out of this without "being on punishment."

Frank took a deep breath. "Let's just suppose, okay? Suppose the doctor who gave Lindsey her asthma medicine last week cheated on his tests. Suppose he cheated on the test dealing with asthma that day? Would it be a big deal?"

Silence.

Angie looked back at her little sister who had drifted asleep. She nodded her head. "Yes."

Frank kissed the top of her head. "Get some sleep." He pulled back the cover as she crawled into bed. He turned off the light and was about to close the door when he heard, "Dad."

"Yes, precious?"

"I'm sorry, it's just…sometime I don't study…sometime… I miss…"

"I know, baby, I know," he cut her off.

"Dad?"

It was Sheila.

"Yes, baby?"

"We miss mom but ..." he could hear the cracking in her small voice, "we're glad we have you."

It took all of his energy to say three words, "I'm glad, too."

He laid his head against his closed bedroom door. Tears slowly rolled down his cheeks as he shook with grief. He began to cry. As his salty tears ran down his cheeks and into the corner of his mouth, he sobbed, "Lord, help me get through this," he whispered. "I miss Annette so much."

Chapter 11

Saturday morning, seventeen minutes before the alarm sounded, Lisa stretched, threw back the comforter and crawled out of bed. She shivered the moment her left foot touched the cold tile floor. She'd forgotten to put down the rug after returning from the Laundromat. One after another she fished her house shoes from under the bed and trotted off to the bathroom. A warm shower was always invigorating.

Afterward, Lisa hung her bath towel on the back of the door. She smiled as she caught her reflection in the bathroom mirror. "Today is the beginning of a new and exciting future," she mused. The words surprised her as they rolled off her tongue.

New job? Yes.

Exciting future? It remained to be seen.

Lisa, an avid reader, was elated to have gotten the job as a clerk in her neighborhood library. The pay was less than she had expected, but the short distance to work offset the lower wages. She could walk to work and save on gas. The added savings could be earmarked to finish decorating her apartment.

Lisa wasn't big on entertaining. It didn't faze her that the living room was empty except for a futon and a small television. The gallery style kitchen had a used card table that she used as an island. Her bedroom contained a twin bed and a three-drawer chest.

As she walked out the front door, she stopped and looked back. In a strange way she felt as though she wasn't just closing a chapter but beginning a brand new book.

*   *   *

Lisa smiled as she walked through the front door. Finally, she had the job she wanted.

"Hi, Lisa; I'm Mrs. Greenfield. Its very unorthodox for an employee to start on Saturday but I wanted your first day to be an easy one," she smiled. "Because we are around the corner from a middle school the weekdays can be very …let's say challenging."

"Thank you," Lisa noted with gratitude.

"Okay. If there are no questions, I'll show you around."

Lisa found Mrs. Greenfield warm and easygoing. She made her first day on the job relaxing. If the first day was an indication of the future Lisa was going to be very happy working there.

At 12:25 p.m. Lisa grabbed her lunch and headed toward the lunchroom. She passed three studious females. The youngest one caught her attention as she skipped to the front desk.

Lisa smiled.

"Hi, girls; I've missed you all. I haven't worked on a Saturday in a long time. How have you all been?" greeted Mrs. Greenfield. Looking around she asked, "No mommy, today?"

Lindsey spoke first. "Mommy's gone to heaven."

Lisa stopped. A lump formed in her throat.

Mrs. Greenfield came around the desk "Girls, I'm so sorry," she said as she bent down.

"We still have daddy." Lindsey added ruefully.

"Yes, you do."

Lisa lost her appetite. She turned and walked back to the desk. Her eyes locked with Mrs. Greenfield's. She believed she could identify with them. Mrs. Greenfield nodded approvingly.

Lisa placed her hand on Lindsey's shoulder. "How can I help you today? Anything in particular?"

Lindsey spoke up. "I want to see where heaven is on the gobe."

"Globe, Lindsey," Shelia corrected, "and it's not on the globe. It's up past the clouds and stars and sun…"

"Well, how do I get to it? How do I get to mommy?" she asked

The question pierced Lisa's heart; she struggled to keep her balance as she fought back tears.

Chapter 12

Frank didn't like working weekends but after being unemployed for a couple of months, he wasn't about to complaint.

For the first night in months, Frank had gotten at least seven hours of sleep. A couple more hours of sleep would have been even better, he thought, as he stretched out his arms and turned over. He pulled his body into a fetal position and reached for the other pillow. The bright sun rays shined between the partially-closed curtains. It had seemed like a short period of time, but Frank knew immediately that he had overslept.

He reached for the clock on the nightstand but it had fallen to the floor. It was 8:32. Frank had set the clock to buzz at seven. He had planned to surprise the girls with a special breakfast. He guessed it was time for a new alarm. As he picked it up, he noticed it hadn't been set.

"We are going to have to hurry this morning," he murmured under his breath as he pulled his underwear from the chest drawer.

"It's after 8:30, ladies. Wake your brother up. I just have two words: Sunday school." Frank yelled as he stuck his head out into the hallway.

Silence.

"The answer will be 'no" the next time they want to go to the movies on a Saturday evening. For the second time this month they can't get up," he fussed as he made his way across the hall.

He tapped lightly on the door, then harder. No response. He pushed the door opened and stopped in his tracks.

The beds were neatly made. Lindsey's headboard was covered with neatly-arranged stuff animals. The room was empty. "I know good and well they are not asleep in the living room. I told them last…"

A voice came from behind startled him. "Looking for us, Dad?" He jumped and turned to see the girls dressed in their Sunday's best. Angie and Sheila looked indifferent, as if there had been no premeditation; however, the mischievous grin on Lindsey's face betrayed their innocent look.

"We'll be down stairs with Marcus when you are ready, dad," Angie informed him. She turned to her sisters and motioned, "Let's go, girls. We don't want to make dad late for Sunday School."

"We sure don't", Sheila agreed, as she quickly put her hand to her mouth to suppress a laugh.

"Sure don't," chimed Lindsey, before asking Sheila, "What's so funny?"

Frank shook his head and chuckled. He had gotten a dose of his own medicine. It was a little bitter in his mouth, but he had to swallow it.

On the drive to church, several times while glancing in the rearview mirror, Frank caught Lindsey and her sisters snickering. Annette often teased Lindsey saying she was like "a broken refrigerator not able to keep anything." Frank pretended not to notice but knew that Lindsey was bubbling over, eager to tell him something. He knew it was a matter of time before "the levee would break."

Marcus, Sheila and Angie jumped out of the car the moment Frank pulled up to the front door of the church.

"I'll be in as soon as I find a parking spot," Frank stated, as Lindsey exited the car.

She looked sad. "What's wrong, honey?" Frank hoped she wasn't sick.

"I wanted to wake you up but Angie said you need to…to take your medicine."

"That's get a taste of my own medicine."

"Huh?"

"Never mind."

"Sheila said we are all in trouble. I didn't do nothing; I'm little."

"Lindsey, Daddy isn't mad. Daddy learned an important lesson today."

"You did? Then, I'm going to give you a happy face when I get home. You learned a lesson like I do at school." And off she went to find her sisters.

As he turned into the parking lot, Frank waited as a homeless woman slowly made her way across the driveway. Something about her walk caught Frank's attention. It was as though one leg was slightly shorter than the other. Her haggard and dirty face made it difficult to tell her age or race. Yet there was something familiar about her. A fisherman hat was pulled down on her forehead. Though the weather was warm she wore a heavy red coat, along with paint-stained sweat pants several sizes too large.

She hobbled across the street while Frank waited patiently. Not once did she look up, not even when a car behind her braked and made a shrieking sound. It grieved Frank's heart that there were so many homeless people in such a rich country like America.

"Girls, where is your sister?" asked Frank as he walked up the sidewalk. His daughters had joined a group of young ladies.

"Isn't she with you?" Sheila retorted.

"No!" answered Frank, opening his hands as if to say, "If she were, would I be asking you?"

"There she is!" pointed one of the girls. "She's talking to that bum lady; she has a new friend."

The sisters laughed but abruptly stopped the moment Frank cleared his throat rather loudly.

"Sorry," said one of the young ladies as she dropped her head.

"She is talking to a homeless woman, not a bum," Frank corrected them. He tilted his head as if to say do you understand.

"Dad, dad, over here!" beckoned Lindsey.

"This is Mrs. Pauley. She used to teach at a Head part," Lindsey told her father as he walked up.

"You mean, Head Start," corrected Frank as he wondered how Lindsey learned so much about the woman in only a few minutes.

"That's what I said. Didn't you Mrs. Pauley, tell him?" she insisted.

"Yes, a long, long time ago," Mrs. Pauley mumbled.

"How are you Mrs. Pauley? My name is Frank." He extended his hand as he introduced himself.

Mrs. Pauley rubbed her hand vigorously against the side of her pants before extending it to Frank. Her hand was rough, Frank smiled politely.

"You have a kind-hearted daughter, Frank." Lindsey smiled as she twisted and turned while holding her dad's hand.

"Yes, she takes after her mom."

Rumbled. Rumbled.

Lindsey grabbed her stomach and apologized. "I am sorry. My stomach always does that, even when I eat. I ate two pancakes. My big sister makes the bestest breakfast in the whole wide world," she said as she stretched out her arms.

"Lindsey, it's she makes the BEST breakfast."

"That's what I said, Dad. What did you have for breakfast, Mr. Pauley?"

She shook her head. "Nothing."

"Your stomach is going to be sounding like a volcano, too," Lindsey offered. "Won't it, Daddy?"

Frank forced a weak smile.

"I know, I know, we can take you to…"

"Lindsey, Lindsey, baby; Mrs. Pauley may not…"

"Aren't you hungry, Mrs. Pauley?" she asked with a genuine concern.

Mrs. Pauley nodded her head in reply to the question, yet her face maintained the determined look of a woman committed to preserving her dignity.

Frank did not want to be late for service. He eased up his jacket sleeve to check his watch and glanced down the street to the nearest fast-food restaurant, which was at the end of the block.

Frank dug into his pocket and pulled out single-dollar bills he had planned to give his daughter to put in the church offering. He counted out six singles and offered them to Mrs. Pauley. She refused them.

"Dad, can we go with her so she doesn't have to eat by herself."

"Come on now, Lindsey," Frank thought to himself, "You are pushing it."

"Mrs. Pauley says she stays by herself—nobody to play with, talk with or watch television with. She says she doesn't have any friends. Can we be her friends just for today, dad?"

Frank looked down into the most compassionate brown eyes he'd ever seen. There was no way he could refuse a simple selfless act.

"Sure, honey; of course we can."

Lindsey turned to Mrs. Pauley and bragged, "See, I told you my dad is the bestest dad in the whole wide world."

"No, it's the best dad, Lindsey."

"I know you are; that's what I said."

"No, I mean…"

"Let's go Mrs. Pauley. We are your friends."

Frank turned and waved to the girls who were across the lawn talking.

"Go on inside; we'll be right back," he instructed them. He tried to show disinterest in the puzzled expressions on their faces.

All through the meal, Frank kept sneaking glances when Mrs. Pauley wasn't looking. He couldn't put his finger on it but he was sure he'd met her somewhere…but where? When?

During the meal Mrs. Pauley responded mostly by nodding or shaking her head. She spoke few words. She ate her food as if it was the first meal she'd had in a while. Frank tried not to stare but it hurt his heart to see her like this. Where was her family? Did she have siblings? Children? Friends?

Lindsey asked question after question. Usually Frank would have stopped her. Honestly, he was glad that he hadn't. They learned that Mrs. Pauley was a widow. She had a daughter but had not seen or talked to her in years. She didn't say why. She didn't know whether she had grandchildren or not. Lindsey smiled when Mrs. Pauley said she wished she had a granddaughter just like her.

Frank couldn't help noticing that Mrs. Pauley had a gentle, kind demeanor. There was a small crescent shape scar near her right eye.

After she had finished, she thanked them for the meal. They watched her slowly make her way across the street. Frank was sure he'd seen her somewhere before. He just couldn't remember where.

Frank and Lindsey watched Mrs. Pauley slowly make her way down the street before they turned and walked back to church. Frank heart was moved with compassion.

"Lindsey, thank you."

"For what, Dad?"

"For teaching me."

"Teach you what?"

"A lot about doing the right thing, honey"

Lindsey looked puzzled but she didn't say anything for a moment.

"Dad?"

"Yes, baby."

"I love Grandma Kate and Grandma Cille, but I wish I could have three grandmas."

"Why, what makes you say that?"

"Then," her voice hung in the air. "Then Mrs. Pauley would have a nice family like us."

"Give me a hug, kid. That's a nice thing to say."

"Dad, I am going to pray that Mrs. Pauley have a nice family just like us do"

"You mean just like we do."

"That's what I said, dad."

He smiled and shook his head, "Me, too, kid; me too."

Frank took two steps and stopped suddenly.

"Wait a minute," shouted Frank. Lindsey froze in her tracks. Frank scanned the street in both directions. With the exceptions of a few late parishioners, the street was empty.

The park! He remembered the woman with the cart. The limp. The scar. He was sure this was the same woman. He remembered the coin purse.

Frank checked his watch as he and Lindsey walked up the steps to the church's front door. Service had started.

"Honk."

"Don't forget to pray for me," someone shouted from a passing car.

Frank recognized Jerome's white Ford Focus as it turned the corner.

"Sure will."

Unlike in the past when he had made fun of Frank going to church every Sunday with Annette and the kids, Frank knew this time, he wasn't teasing.

Even though, Frank had tried to assure him that it was his "personal" decision, Jerome wasn't convinced. However, after Annette's death, he had confessed to Frank that he'd watched him during the funeral and the weeks, months that followed. He had seen with his own eyes and was, now, convinced that it was his faith that had sustained him.

Quietly and respectfully, Frank and Lindsey slipped into the back pew.

*   *   *

Frank stopped at the bottom of the stairs with a smile spread across his face. It was such a nice quiet Sunday afternoon, much like it had been in the past. Shelia and Angie were cleaning up the kitchen; Marcus and Lindsey were sprawled across the living room floor playing Uno. The house was peaceful. His countenance fell as his heart longed for Annette.

"The score is two to two. How many games are we playing?" Lindsey asked.

"Five," Marcus answered.

"I'm going to get some chips; be right back," Lindsey stated and turned her cards over.

"Bring me a bag, please," Marcus requested, as he reached for Lindsey's cards.

"Don't do it!" said Frank.

Marcus looked up into his father's disapproving face.

"Sorry!" Marcus apologized.

"For what? Wanting to cheat or getting caught?"

"Remember, if you have to cheat to win you are a bigger loser. Others may not know but you'll always know."

"What's wrong?" Lindsey wanted to know after she saw the look on Marcus's face.

"Nothing, baby; your brother and I are just talking about life. Right, son?"

"Right," Marcus announced. "I'm going to beat you fair and square, little sister."

Frank gave him a thumb's up.

"No, you're not," Lindsey bellowed, and placed the winning "Uno" card in front of them.

"Let's play Tic Tac Toe next," said Lindsey.

"Great. I love this game."

"Yep, me, too"

In the past Marcus had beaten Lindsey every time they played. He was confident that he was going to do it again. He did not know that his father had taught Lindsey how to play the game.

Frank pulled up a chair. He wanted to see if Lindsey remembered what he had taught her.

"I want to go first," she insisted.

"Sure; ladies first; even young ladies," Marcus deferred, not the least bit threatened.

X...O...X...O...X...O

"My win," Lindsey announced and danced a gig.

"One more," Marcus pleaded.

"Okay."

"This time I'm going first"

"Okay."

Tie.

O..X..O..X..O..X

Tie

X..O..X..O..X..O

"I'm done," he conceded and got up.

Great job, sis," he called as he climbed the stairs.

"Thanks."

Frank gave her a high five.

Chapter 13

"No, honey; I don't think that's appropriate for your age." Or any age, he thought to himself. Frank smiled as he remembered his mom's (a woman from the hippie era) joke about Sheila's taste in clothes. She'd often said that Sheila's clothes were "far out"—like from another planet.

He shook his head again as she held up two more dresses.

"No, and no."

She held them up and examined them closely. With the naivete of a preteen, she asked, "Why? What? This is what all of the girls at my school is wearing. This is the 'in' look, dad," she reasoned.

"Honey, look at how low cut they are; and they are short."

"Daddy, what can I buy then?" she asked in frustration.

"Anything that that's not so low that others can see your chest, or so short that you have to pull up on it when you sit down, or so tight that people can tell whether you are wearing briefs or boxers."

Sheila and Lindsey giggled.

"You don't understand," She threw her hand in the air. "You don't know what's in style."

"Baby, I do understand. And, yes, a woman can take you shopping."

For real?" Sheila's face lit up.

"For real; I'll ask Grandma Kate to take you tomorrow."

Her face dropped. "Okay, okay, I'll keep looking."

Chapter 14

Frank dreamed that he was being stared down by a tall bear. In a cold sweat, he opened his eyes. Lindsey stood over him; her face almost touched his nose. She giggled and said "You sound like the wind Daddy."

Irritated, he asked "Did you knock Lindsey?"

"No, dad; I didn't want to wake you up. So I just stood here until you woke up."

"Dad, I'm bored," Lindsey lamented as she climbed upon the bed. Frank stuffed his pillow behind his back and sat up. As he rubbed his eye, he asked, "What time is it?"

"It's time for the cartoons to go off," Lindsey answered.

"Okay, so what do you want to do today?"

She shrugged her shoulders, "I don't know.

"Zoo?"

"Naah."

"Movies?"

"Naah."

"Park?"

"Naah."

"L-I-n-d-s-e-y, don't say 'naah.' The word is 'no.' Now look…"

"I know. Let's go to the library. They have storytelling on Saturday."

Frank didn't hesitate—the library was free, and it was near.

"Library it is. Get your library card while I get dressed."

"Yeaaaaaaaaaaaaaaaaaa, we're going to the liberry!"

"Li-br-a-ry!!!!!!!!!"

"That's what I said."

∗   ∗   ∗

He looked around the room in amazement. The local library was a far cry from the one in his old neighborhood. He readily understood why the girls enjoyed visiting; it looked like a fun place. In the children section was a large, colorful, alphabet rug that covered the center of the room. Around the perimeter were circles for the children to sit during story -time. The entire library was filled with books and bright colored chairs.

An estimated twenty children sat with rapt attention during storytelling hour. As Mrs. Jones, the grandmotherly- looking lady took her seat, the children got comfortable. Lindsey ran to the bright colored L to claim her seat. Frank decided to spend the hour reading sport magazines. He chuckled when he remembered that the entire library where he grew up was smaller than the local library's children section. He inquired about the card catalog only to be told everything was computerized.

Annette had always taken the children to the library. It had been about fifteen years since he'd visited a library. He wouldn't be able to find anything without assistance.

"Excuse me," whispered a soft feminine voice behind him.

"Sure," whispered Frank as he stepped aside.

As the young lady passed, her sweater caught Frank's attention—Annette had an identical sweater. But it was her flawless skin, long thick lashes over clear brown eyes, and cute dimples that held his attention.

The young lady thumbed through several rows of books, and looked up to find Frank staring. He was embarrassed. "I'm sorry. I didn't mean to stare. It's just your sweater reminded me of someone. Ahhh. Can I help you find something?"

"No, thank you," Lisa replied politely, "I think I can manage."

"Librarian, lady, can you help me find a book about dinosaurs?" a little boy asked as he tugged on her jacket.

"I sure can." She looked at Frank and entreated, "Excuse me." As she followed the lad, over her shoulder she whispered, "Thanks for the offer."

Was that a giggle he heard?

While waiting on Lindsey, Frank thumbed through several magazines before deciding to check out a book on DIY projects. He needed to fix the dripping bathroom faucet and the torn screen in the front door. First, he would have to get a library card.

** * *

Frank read the book that weekend and returned it the following Monday after work.

Okay, who was he fooling? The truth was that he wanted to see the librarian again. He couldn't get her out of his mind.

With his new library card, he decided to go to the children's section. Since he was there, he reasoned, he might as well check out a book for Lindsey.

"Uhhhmm," Frank cleared his throat as he nervously and lightly tapped his card on the desk.

The young lady looked up, recognized him and smiled.

"Okay, the joke was on me." He confessed. "I…"

The phone rang across the room. Mrs. Greenfield answered it.

"Ms. Carter, it's for you; It's Mr. Carter," she chuckled.

"Excuse me, please; it will take just a moment," as she turned to answer the phone.

Frank nodded.

"Hi, what's up?"

Frank browsed through the stack of magazines on the counter. He could hear the conversation.

"I'll be home around seven," Ms. Carter noted.

Frank felt foolish and wanted to avoid further embarrassment. He hurried away before she could get off the phone, he left his card behind.

"Sorry, that was my …," she turned to an empty counter.

Her smile faded.

Disappointed, she scanned the room. He was about to exit the building.

"Mr. ...," she whispered as she caught up with him at the door. "Ah, Mr. Hall. You left your card," observing his name.

"Thanks." He stammered. "I apologize. I shouldn't have left like that but when I overheard you talking to your husband... well I felt like I'd made a fool out of myself again."

"My husband...what do you? Oh, you mean," she pointed to the desk. "You mean the phone call?"

"Yeah."

"Oh, you mean the mister part?"

"Yeah, I wasn't eavesdropping...I mean ...I just overheard you."

"That was my neighbor. He always calls when he needs something from the store. He is elderly so I don't mind. He calls so often, the head librarian teases me sometime.'

A wave of relief rolled over Frank. He displayed a smile while desperately trying to hold back a broad grin. "Oh."

"I'm Lisa Carter," she introduced herself and extended her hand.

"Frank Hall." He didn't realize he was still holding her hand until she gently pulled it away.

"When do you get off?" he asked.

She glanced at her watch. It was 6:06.

"6 minutes ago. Hold on, I'll be right back"

She stopped and looked back. Frank Hall. The name was vaguely familiar.

Butterflies were in his stomach. No one had captured his attention like this...other than Annette.

He stepped out of the doorway as a group of giggling teenaged boys and girls entered. Frank smiled. He felt pretty youthful himself at the moment.

"Sorry, it took so long. I had to look over some invoices. There is a diner across from the park. How about some coffee?" she asked, as she pulled her sweater around her shoulders.

"Sounds good."

After telling her about his children coming to the library often, he was not surprise that she knew them, especially Lindsey.

"You have wonderful daughters and a son, although I must admit I rarely see your son."

"Thanks, they are my heart."

"Lindsey told me that you are her "bestest" friend. I thought that was cute."

They strolled along the street and talked about the upcoming elections, the weather, and general casual conversations. Frank enjoyed each moment.

Frank reached for her hand as they crossed the street. Her hand was soft, which reminded him of Annette's. He dropped it the moment they stepped on the curb. He noticed her puzzled look but ignored it. He felt like he was...like he was being unfaithful to Annette.

Lisa put her hands into her pockets. She'd lost her train of thought, so she was quiet as they walked into the restaurant.

"Do you mind if we sit near the window?" Lisa asked as she took her purse off her shoulder.

"That's fine," he replied, as he helped her with her sweater.

A young waitress dressed in a crisp white blouse and black slacks walked up to them.

"Hi, I'm Jan. I will be your server. What can I get you?" she asked and pulled a pen and pad from her apron pocket.

"Hi, two coffees and…," he waited for her to add on.

"Just coffee for me," Lisa added, as she scooted near the window.

"Two coffees and a blueberry muffin," ordered Frank. He noticed the space next to her, but did not want to be presumptuous. He decided to sit across from her. Lisa slid back to the middle of the seat. He realized that she had wanted him to sit next to her.

"I saw your son in the park. So where are the girls today?"

"Huh?"

"The girls, where are they today?"

"Oh, they are with their grandparents."

There was silence.

"Frank, are you okay?"

"Yes; I'm sorry, Lisa. You see, my wife……,"

She gently patted his hand. "I know, I know, Frank. You don't have to talk about it."

He looked puzzled. How could she know what he was going to say?

"Lindsey told me her mom passed. She just came over to the desk and started talking one day. Now that I look back, it was coincidental. I was feeling sad when she came up to the desk one day. You see, I haven't seen my mom in years. I don't even know if she's… Well, Lindsey and I sort of helped each other through that difficult moment."

Lisa continued. "I remember her smile; her eyes twinkled. I remember the three of us going to the park. We would swing and slide for hours. In my teen years I remember engaging in a lot of girl talks. It always seemed like the sun was shining. I remember a lot of laughter. Not just mine but mom and dad's as well. Then, when I was sixteen, while they were on their way home from shopping, a drunk driver turned the wrong way and collided with their vehicle. My father died the next day from internal bleeding. Mom walked away with a small scar and a limp. It was hard on her. The guilt. It was clear that a part of her died with my dad. She became withdrawn. Aunt Dean moved in with us to help out. Mom started staying alone in her room more and more. Then, one day in my senior year, mom withdrew her small savings. She left it on the bed. We never saw or heard from her again."

"But it wasn't her fault; it just happened," Frank analyzed.

Lisa nodded. "I know. Everybody tried to get her to see that. Aunt Dean tried to get her some therapy but," she shook her head, "she wouldn't." She shrugged her shoulders and took a deep breath.

"I am so sorry," Frank consoled.

"My Aunt Dean and Uncle Charlie are the greatest. I was always close to them. They gave me all I could ask for…. except….," her voice trailed off. A quizzical expression appeared across her face. "You know, it's as though mom is watching me. I mean, I can't explain it… it's silly but I'll be walking down the street and feel like she's there. She was so beautiful. We'd go to the park every Saturday. We'd have so much fun."

"That's it. That's where I remember Mrs. Pauley. The park! The lady in the park! The scar. The limp. Could Mrs. Pauley, a homeless woman, be Lisa's mom?"

Frank couldn't say anything yet. He could be wrong, but he was determined to learn more.

"I always carry this picture," Lisa opened her wallet, "just to have my parents close to me.

I have closure with my father; I know what happened ….but with my mom … just leaving with no goodbye…nothing…," her voice trailed off.

"I am sorry," Frank repeated. "I didn't mean to…"

"No, that's alright. As crazy as it might seem, I love to talk about her. I miss her so much."

Lisa leaned over and whispered. It was as though she was embarrassed or hesitant to mention it.

"You know, sometime I have this feeling that she is watching me," she shivered. "I know it's nothing," she shrugged her shoulders. "I hope you don't think I'm paranoid."

"No, I know you are not."

He sounded so confident, until she eyed him suspiciously. "How can you be so sure?"

"Because I have good judgment," he quickly added.

Frank looked down at the picture. Could it be her? He wasn't sure. But he was sure to find out.

Chapter 15

Frank splashed cold water on his face, and patted it dry. He stopped and looked intensely at the man in the mirror. This time, the reflection he saw; a well-groomed, well-rested man who had regained his weight, made him smile.

Frank looked down at his stomach. Not only had he regained his weight but had picked up extra. He pinched his love handles. He'd have to start going to the gym.

It had been four months since he and Lisa first had coffee at the diner. It had become a weekend tradition. Once when Lisa was late, one of the waitresses had told him that they had noticed the chemistry between him and Lisa. She thought they made a cute couple. One of the male servers even warned him to not let her get away. Frank had agreed that Lisa was a special woman, and that he had no intention of losing her.

He noticed the time and headed down stairs whistling "Dixie." Lisa was working this Saturday so Frank had planned to meet her during her lunch. At the bottom of the stairs he could see the sun rays stream into the living room window. He also noticed the tree branches swaying back and forth. He decided to get a jacket out of the hall closet.

He heard the children in the kitchen but did not want to interrupt, so he headed out the front door. As he opened the door, he yelled out, "Be back in an hour or so."

Silence.

Bewildered, he closed the door and walked to the kitchen. The children sat at the table looking gloomy.

"What's up? Why all the long faces?"

Silence.

"Anything we need to talk about?" he didn't have a clue. He hung his coat on the back of the chair and sat down.

"Okay, who wants to go first?"

"I will because I'm the youngest," Lindsey volunteered.

"Okay."

"Shanta said…"

"Are you going to marry Ms. Lisa?" Marcus blurted out.

"Dad, aren't you happy with us?" Lindsey asked with the innocence of a five year old.

"Of course, I am. So, is this what the long faces are about?" he asked relieved.

"Kids, before I marry anyone, I will discuss it with you all, okay." He looked at his watch and added, "It's five minutes after eight; I have to go. We will talk later."

"We won't let her take mommy's place," Lindsey cried out.

"We don't need a mom. Why can't it just be us?" asked Shelia.

Angie was very quiet. Each time one of her siblings spoke, she tried to get their attention with her facial expressions.

A loud noise came from the porch. Frank opened the door to investigate. He was astonished to see Lisa backing her car out of the drive. At the bottom of the steps, was an overturned flowerpot.

*   *   *

"Lisa! We need to talk," Frank whispered. Lisa stamped return cards and placed them in the appropriate books. Frank leaned against her desk. She looked up.

"Not now; I'm busy."

"When?"

"Later."

"Later, w-h-e-n?" He persisted, which caused Mrs. Greenfield to stop typing and look up over her glasses.

"What time are you getting off tonight?"

Lisa shrugged her shoulders as if to say she didn't know.

"Seven?"

"Eight?"

"Nine?"

"Frank, please go home. The girls will be worrying about you," she pleaded.

"And if I go I'll be worrying about YOU," he countered. He quickly added, "I'll be outside." He turned and walked away disappointed.

Mrs. Greenfield stopped typing as Frank walked to the front door. She watched Lisa over the top of her glasses for a moment before getting up.

"Punch out at seven," she instructed Lisa without an explanation.

"But you asked me to stay until nine; remember?"

"Look, young lady, you can't make all the overtime. I'm staying until nine. It's five minutes until seven; get your things," she ordered, trying to sound stern.

Lisa pulled her purse out of the cabinet drawer, turned to her boss and smiled.

"Thanks, Mrs. Greenfield."

"For what? Go on, get out of here!" she blushed.

"Yes, ma'am," Lisa retorted, as she backed into the desk and sent a can of pens and pencils tumbling to the floor.

"I got it; go on," Mrs. Greenfield laughed.

"Thank you so much," Lisa said, as she turned into the cart she was working on and caused a row of books to fall to the floor.

"Go on; I got it," Mrs. Greenfield chuckled and waved her away.

A group of teens across the aisle had witnessed the scene and burst into laughter. Embarrassed, Lisa hurried out the building.

The parking lot was full; she couldn't see Frank's car. She held the rail and slowly made her way down the steps. She had hoped he would be waiting, no matter how late she would get off. She shivered—not from the cold but from anxiety. She threw a sweater over her shoulders and tried to comfort herself.

"Lisa, hold up." Her heart skipped a beat as she recognized Frank's voice.

She turned to see him running toward her. "I thought you would be coming out the side door, near the bus stop. I almost missed you."

She was so glad that he hadn't.

"Do you mind if I drive you home?"

"It's only two blocks."

"O-k-a-y. Mind if I walk you home?"

"What about your car?" she asked.

"I'll walk back and get it. I don't care as long as I get a chance to spend a few minutes with you," he observed.

"Okay, okay, you can drive me home."

The drive was too short for a long conversation, so they rode in silence. Frank parked in front of Lisa's apartment and turned off the motor. As he turned to speak, she quickly raised her hand to silence him.

She carefully unhooked the clash on the bracelet he had given her a week earlier for her birthday. With her right hand she picked up his left one and dropped it in his palm. She wanted to tell him how she felt but the words wouldn't come.

As he looked longingly at her, his eyes asked, "What does this mean? What are you saying?"

"I'm not trying to take your wife's place. I'm not trying to take the girls' mother's place."

"Oh, Lisa, I'm sorry. I'm sorry. I know you heard them in the kitchen?"

She dropped her head and nodded.

Frank laid his head on the back of the seat, slowly ran his fingers through his hair, and let out a sigh. At daybreak, he had felt like the happiest guy in town. He had regained much of the joy he had lost. Now, just when he was beginning to live again, the woman who had restored the joy seemed prepared to take it away.

Frank wanted to reach for her hand; yet he gripped the steering wheel as he searched for the right words to say.

"I'm sorry you had to hear that but if you had waited, you would have heard me tell the kids that no one is trying to take or can take their mom's place. Their mother was a beautiful, caring wonderful person whom I loved dearly; I could never forget her, never. Even if I wanted to, I couldn't. I see her in Sheila's smile, Angie's walk, and Lindsey's big heart. But I wanted them to know there has been a void in my heart since their mom died. You fill that void. No matter what happens or don't happen I'll always remember you. Although I've only known you a few months, you have become a big part of my life. Lisa, I love my children very much but," he wanted to say, "I also love you and I don't want to lose you," but he stopped short of saying it.

She wanted him to finish the sentence but he didn't. She forced a weak smile and picked up her things.

"Good bye, Frank," Lisa said without making eye contact.

"Lisa, wait; please."

She fumbled with the door lock before making her exit. Frank wasn't sure but he thought he heard crying. A part of him wanted to run after her, to comfort her, but if he did, then what? He wasn't sure of what to say. He just wasn't sure.

He turned the key in the ignition and headed home.

Chapter 16

Lindsey burst into Frank's room and flopped down on the side of his bed. "Dad, who is going to comb my hair?" She held the comb and brush.

"Where are your sisters?" he asked as he stretched and yawned.

"They have gone swimming, remember?"

"I guess so," he scratched his head and sat up. "You know you don't have to comb it every day."

"Mom combed my hair every day," Lindsey replied and placed the comb in her father's hand.

He sat up on the side of the bed. Lindsey's hair stood out like a Diana Ross' wig. He hated to hear people use the terms "good hair" and "bad hair" but as he struggled to untangle the curls and knots in Lindsey's mane, he definitely realized that some hair textures were a lot easier to manage than others.

This was one of those times he wished he had been paying attention while Annette fixed the girls' hair.

Frank picked up a hand full of hair but did not have a clue as to what to do next.

"Dad, can I have a French roll?"

"No."

"Why?"

"That style is a little grown up. There will be plenty of time for that when you are older." Besides, he thought, I wouldn't know how to make one any way.

"Are you going to make my pony tails with rubber bands like Angie does or scrunchies like mom use to make?"

"With scrunchies like your mom, of course."

Frank looked down at the hair box she was holding on her lap. It was filled with every color of barrettes, ribbons, and things for her hair. Somewhere in the pile, he was sure, were scrunchies.

Lindsey saw her father's look of despair and picked up two scrunchies and gave them to him.

Of course, thought Frank, as he smoothed the wrinkles from two elastic bands of fabric only to see them crinkle up again.

He twisted and turned the scrunchies, trying to figure out what to do with them. He was flabbergasted but managed a smile. Annette had always said, "Look on the bright side; there is always a silver lining." In this case, he was sure it was the fact that he had three daughters instead of four.

After much brushing, combing, twisting and untwisting, Frank was pleased with the result. The big question was would Lindsey be also? Frank nervously waited as Lindsey walked over to the dresser to check out her hair. He knew Lindsey would be honest; she was sometimes brutally honest.

"Wow, thanks. These are just like mom used to make," announced Lindsey as she looked into the mirror and turned from side to side.

* * *

After returning from swimming, Angie and Sheila volunteered to cook dinner, and had gone online to find easy recipes for their favorite dishes. After much dissension, a compromise was made. They agreed on Lindsey's favorites: scalloped potatoes, baked chicken tenders and a garden salad. Shanta had come over to help and ask if she could spend the night, again.

As usual, after dinner, Marcus found much to criticize. Frank, however, assured the girls that his criticisms were unfounded. The meal was delectable.

Frank and Marcus cleaned up the kitchen before relaxing in the living room to watch a basketball game.

"Well, Dad."

"I know, I know."

The one with the losing team had promised to straighten up the living room after the game. Marcus saluted his dad and headed up the stairs.

"Next time, son."

"Sure, that's what you said after the last three games."

Actually it had been four games but there was no need to remind his gloating son, Frank thought, as he picked a few pieces of popcorn off the floor and grabbed the empty glasses.

As Frank headed to his room, he tapped on Marcus's door—"next time son, next time."

"Sure, Dad, sure."

Frank tapped on the girls' door. "Girls."

"Who is it?" Shanta asked.

"Come in," Sheila said.

"I just wanted to say thank you again, ladies; a wonderful meal.'

"You welcome, Po.... I mean, positively, you are welcome."

Frank shook his head and closed the door. "Lights out by ten," he added.

He heard Sheila whisper something; Shanta replied, "I keep forgetting."

It had been a long day. Frank threw his shirt on the chair and decided to stretch out for a minute before he took a shower. He clicked on the television. He suspected, as Annette always said, in a few minutes, the television would be watching him.

"Pops!"

"Yesssss, Shanta?"

"Make Lindsey get out of my Kool-Aid," she begged.

"Lindsey, now I know you know better than that. There's a whole case of pops in the pantry."

Laughter spilled out of the room.

"Go get the spritz from the bathroom, Lindsey?" pleaded Angie as she styled Shanta's hair.

"What's wrong with your legs?" asked Lindsey as she continued combing her doll's hair.

"Lindsey, please!" she pleaded. "Oh, forget it. I'll go myself."

Angie threw a pillow at Lindsey. "I'd sell you for ten dollars," she hissed and walked out of the room.

"No, you wouldn't."

"Yeah, you are right. I probably wouldn't get but two."

Shanta giggled. Lindsey licked out her tongue and threw a pillow at Shanta's head.

"Pops!"

"Okay, Shanta. If you call me 'Pops' one more…," yelled Frank from across the hall before closing his bedroom door.

"See what you did?" she blamed Lindsey.

"You know Dad hate for you to call him 'Pops.' Why do you do it? He's going to stop you from sleeping over."

"That's what I call my old man."

"Yeah, but you keep forgetting one thing."

"What?"

"My dad is not your old man."

"You think he's really mad at me?"

"No, he's not mad but he doesn't like the way you don't consider his feelings. He's not going to keep allowing it after he has told you several times."

"I won't do it again; I promise."

Angie shrugged her shoulders. "Don't tell me, tell Dad."

"Can I have a sheet of paper and use your pen, please?"

Angie tore a sheet from a tablet and gave it to her. Shanta scribbled on the paper, went across the hall and slipped it under Mr. Hall's door.

Hearing a scratching sound, Frank reached over and turned on the lamp. Someone was slowly pushing a folded sheet of paper underneath his door. He smiled. Lindsey was always leaving him hearts with the words I LOVE YOU scribbled on it.

He unfolded the note, expecting the usual terms of affection, but, to his dismay, it was an apology from Shanta. It read:

I'm sorry, Mr. Hall

I promise I won't do it again. I didn't mean any harm.

You treat me nice; I would never do anything mean.

Shanta

Frank felt ashamed. With all the pressure from the job maybe he had overreacted.

Frank knocked on the girl's door.

"Come in," Angie encouraged.

"Shanta, I'm sorry. I didn't mean to sound mean. It's just… Hey, give me a hug, daughter #4."

She dashed across the room and gave him a big hug "It's okay, Po…" He felt her tense as she kept her head buried in his chest.

Frank shook his head and patted her back. "It's okay; at least, you are working on it."

Chapter 17

"Hi, Dad!" shouted Sheila over the noise from the vacuum cleaner.

"Hi, Sheila; Shanta," Frank responded, as he turned it off.

Sheila took Shanta's coat and hung it in the hall closet.

"We are going to get a snack; you want one, dad?" she asked as she closed the closet door.

"No, thanks; I had a late lunch at work," Frank answered, while he wrapped the cord around the vacuum cleaner's handle. "Hey, I saw your book report on the table. That's great honey. I'm proud of you. I knew you could do it." He picked up the appliance and gave her a high five. She missed his hand, and he had to give her another one before he headed for the stairs.

"Didn't you get a C on your paper?" asked Shanta

"Yeah." Sheila proudly admitted. Shanta looked confused.

"What's wrong?"

"Nothing, I guess."

"What?" Sheila persisted. She knew her friend well enough to know she had something to say.

"Why you say it like that?"

"It's just… I mean … when I bring a B home, my pops asks me why I didn't try harder.

Your dad gets excited over a… a C."

"It's not that he gets excited over a C. I mean if I get a C in math, he may put me on punishment because I love math and generally get an A, but when it comes to writing a book report, I don't know what to write. The last time I got a D. Want a pop?

"Only, if it's a cola."

"Sorry, we only have grape," Sheila countered, turning around from the fridge.

"On second thought; I'll take it."

*   *   *

Frank placed the vacuum cleaner in the hall closet and pushed open the door to his bedroom. To his surprise, Lindsey was sprawled across the bed with several of her dolls and stuff animals. "I'm watching television with you, Dad."

"Ooookay," Frank agreed, not knowing what else to say. Lindsey's self-invitation, however, had come at an inopportune time.

Lindsey gave him a pillow. He smiled and stretched out beside her.

"Isn't this fun, Dad?" she asked.

Any other day it would be but not today

Frank smiled and kissed the top of her head. He loved being a father.

The minute Lindsey announced that she was going to get some juice, Frank rushed across the hall to the girls' room.

"Angie, I need a teeny-weenie favor."

"Sure, Dad, but it's going to cost you," Angie took off her headphones to listen.

Frank was not amused. He stopped dead in his tracks and, without a word, gave her "the look."

Angie backpedaled. "Just kidding, Dad; just kidding."

"I have to make out these checks and get them in the mail tomorrow. Lindsey went down stairs to get some juice. When she comes back up I want you to wait five minutes and then come get her. I need one hour to finish."

"Ah, Dad; that's a BIG favor."

"Angie!"

"Okay, okay; I'll do it."

"Thanks, I really need to finish these checks."

Frank turned to see Lindsey standing in the hallway.

"Did you get your juice?" he asked wondering how much of the conversation she had heard.

"No, I was in the bathroom. I had to use it."

He stood, not knowing what to say. Angie came to his rescue.

"Lindsey, why don't you help me with my new puzzle?" she suggested, pulling a box from the closet shelf.

"Okay," Lindsey accepted. "Will it keep me busy for one hour?" she asked.

Chapter 18

Frank called his boss early Monday morning and requested a personal day. Lindsey had wanted to "sleep in Mommy's bed like before." Frank woke up feeling as if he'd been in a fight. There had been jabs, head butts, and knees in his side throughout the night. He stretched out exhausted on the sofa with the remote control and was fast asleep within minutes.

"Stop, Jermaine!"

Frank jumped straight up. His eyes zoomed in on the clock. It was 3:36 p.m. He pulled the curtains back and peered out. In front of the house, Angie was trying to wrestle out of the grips of one of her classmate's arms.

"No, stop now; I'm not playing. You're hurting my arm."

Frank could barely control himself. He swung open the door. The children froze, surprised to see him. The indignation on Frank's face caused the young man's initial embarrassment to quickly morph into fear.

"Hi, Mr. Hall, I was just playing. I'll see you tomorrow, Angie." Jermaine said with a weak smile and hastened out of the yard.

"Wait, Jermaine."

Frank realized he didn't have his wallet. He turned to Angie. "do you have a few dollars; I need you to go to the store for me."

"Yes—to get what, dad?"

"Some …some…some, ah, coffee creamer."

"For your coffee?" she knew he drank his coffee black.

"No. Auntie Barbara."

"Is she here?"

"No, but she'll be here for Christmas."

Christmas was months away but Angie knew her father. She laid her book bag on the steps. As she passed Jermaine, she looked out the corner of her eye and saw the look of terror on his face.

"Jermaine. We need to talk."

Jermaine glanced around. No one was in sight other than Angie and she was going in the opposite direction. Where was the old lady next door who was always at the window or on the porch?

Frank held the door opened and beckoned for Jermaine.

Jermaine stepped up onto the porch as beads of sweat rolled down his temple and into his ear. He felt like a sheep led to the slaughter as a scene from an old movie about a convict walking down a long corridor to the electric chair flashed before him. He slowly walked into the living room.

Frank closed the door. Or did he slam it?

Jermaine wiped his sticky palms along side of his legs. He tried to swallow but his throat was parched.

*   *   *

Halfway down the block, Angie looked back. The yard was empty. Her concern turned to consternation. She hurried as fast as she could to the neighborhood store.

Minutes later, Angie rushed through the front door, the living room was empty. The house was quiet. Hearing movement, she head to the kitchen. Frank was sitting at the table. Surprisingly, he was alone. Angie sat the creamer canister on the table; she hadn't waited for the cashier to bag it.

"Dad…. ah… is Jermaine okay?" she had to ask.

"Yes. I mean, why wouldn't he be?"

"Well, I mean…"

"Honey, I know he's one of your friends. But, as a young lady, don't allow young men to disrespect you, pull on you. And honey, when you say no… mean No. When you say stop… mean STOP!"

She nodded and headed up the stairs.

Frank called out. "Honey, I didn't mean to embarrass you."

"That's okay. I was more concerned about Jermaine," she confessed.

"You had a right to be," Frank mumbled.

"Huh? What you say?" asked Sheila.

"It was nothing."

Chapter 19

"Happy birthday!" a loud chorus emanated from the hallway.

Frank turned over and fell out the bed. He landed on the floor with a thud. He got back in bed and propped his head upon some pillows.

"Come in," he encouraged.

Frank wiped sleep from his eyes while his daughters beamed. Angie held a tray with eggs, bacon and toast; Sheila held a large gift; and Lindsey held a glass of orange juice and a card.

Frank tucked the sheet under his legs as he propped the pillows behind his back.

"Whose birthday is it?" he teased looking at Lindsey.

"It's yours, Daddy. You forgot? Today is Oct.11th?"

"They said as you get old, the mind is the first thing to go," Marcus observed, as he walked into the room.

"Watch it, son," Frank shot back.

The girls all giggled.

Frank took the tray from Angie and sat on the bed. Lindsey sat the juice on the nightstand.

"This is from Angie and me." Sheila offered the box to her father and looked at Lindsey. "Lindsey wanted to buy her gift by herself."

"Dad, this is from me." Lindsey pulled out a small wrapped package from her pocket. "I bought it by myself. Sheila took me to the store but I picked it out by myself.

"You sure did," Sheila co-signed, quickly distancing herself from the gift.

"We will save the best gift for last," Marcus noted with fanfare. He held up a big, square-wrapped package. They all looked surprised. Marcus generally bought a package of gum or candy. He always rationalized that it was the thought that counted; everyone knew he was stingy. Frank fought back tears. Annette had always celebrated Frank's birthday with the children. With her departure, he wasn't expecting it this year. It was a bittersweet moment

"Open mine first, Daddy!"

"Of course, the youngest always come first," Frank acquiesced to Lindsey's satisfaction. She beamed with delight as she dismissively tilted her head toward her sisters and brother.

Frank shook the gift. Not a sound. He maintained his cheerful façade, as Lindsey smilingly looked on. He twisted the package and held it up. He studied the gift. Not a clue.

"You can't guess," Lindsey beamed, "You'll never guess in a million years."

Sheila looked at Angie. They both nodded. She got that right.

A tie?"

"No!"

"Socks?"

"Handkerchiefs?"

"Noooooooo; open it, Daddy," Lindsey incited.

"Okay, okay. I don't know what this is," Frank confessed, as he unwrapped the gift.

"See, I told you; you wouldn't guess," Lindsey giggled.

Frank held up a package of antacids.

Angie observed her father's perplexed expression and decided to explain.

"Lindsey heard you tell Grandma that your heart was aching."

"These will help your heart, Daddy!" Lindsey gushed.

Frank buried his face into Lindsey's shoulder and gave her a long hug. He needed time to compose his emotions.

"Thank you, baby."

"Open our present, Daddy!" Sheila implored.

"Okay." He laid the antacids on the bed.

The neatly wrapped silver box was topped with a golden bow. The card read: From Sheila and Angie. They eagerly watched his facial expression, and he didn't disappoint. "Oh, my, I can't believe it. I love it! How did you know this is what I needed?" he asked as he held up a 7-in-1 screw-driver set."

"We just guessed." Sheila answered.

"Thank you; thank both of you." They beamed in delight.

"Okay, now it's time for the best gift of all. Hold your seat belts, ladies. Prepare to be amazed," Marcus crowed.

With the theatrics and histrionics of a magician, he pulled a lovely, navy blue sweater out of the box. They were amazed that he'd spent more than a couple of dollars on a gift.

"Where did you get the money?" asked Angie, recognizing the label.

"I bathe the dogs for Mrs. Green every Saturday."

"Group hug, group hug," Frank announced, as he beckoned for Marcus.

"Ahhh, Dad; that's for kids," Marcus lamented, before he reluctantly joined the group.

Frank looked at his plate. "Mmmm, let me grab my robe. I want to eat this meal in the dining room, where I can savor it." He waited for them to leave the room. Angie grabbed the tray, Marcus grabbed the glass of juice, and the children headed down stairs.

After they exited, Frank quickly tied his belt and made his way down the stairs. His three daughters were sitting at the table with broad smiles as he pulled out a chair. Marcus had gone to his room.

He hadn't notice the rose from the garden. It extended from beneath the napkin. A lump welled up in his throat. It was what Annette did on his birthday.

"Thank you, girls. This is one of the best birthdays I've ever had."

"For real?" Lindsey asked.

"Come here," he gave her a big hug and admitted, "for real!"

The girls sat with him until he finished his breakfast. He ate every crumb even the burnt edge of the toast. The girls were pleased.

Honk! It was Shanta's mom picking them up for school.

"Marcus, let's go or you'll going to have to walk to school," reminded Angie.

"Here I come" he charged down the stairs and out of the front door.

"No running in the house," Frank reminded.

"See you later, Dad."

"Bye, Dad!"

"Bye, Dad!"

"Hey, hey girls! Hold up a minute," Frank called from the kitchen.

"Give me another hug," He requested with outstretched arms.

"Why?" asked Lindsey.

"Do I have to have a reason to get a hug from my beautiful daughters?" he asked as he twisted her ponytail.

As the girls walked out the front door, Frank recalled an incident that transpired about a year before Annette's death.

He had gone out with two of his former classmates. They started shooting pool and time had slipped by. He had told Annette that he would be home around midnight. It was 2:30 a.m. when he noticed the time. By the time he got home it was 3:15. He was prepared for the "lecture." He knew he had it coming. Annette met him at the door with a hug, relieved that he was safe. She exhaled, "You just never know."

Chapter 20

It had been six months since he met Lisa, but it felt like he'd known her all of his life. In so many ways she was like Annette, yet each possessed her own distinctive quality. Lisa, quiet and reserved, masked her emotions. Frank was persuaded it had a lot to do with her growing up without a mother or father. Annette, in contrast, was more expressive. Her sense of security initially attracted him.

He smiled and remembered the first day he met Annette.

He had taken the train downtown for an interview. Unfamiliar with the downtown area, he had gotten turned around. He wasn't sure whether he was supposed to go north or south, east or west, to get to the interview.

As he walked along the streets, gazing at the skyscrapers, he bumped into a beautiful young lady, which caused her to spill coffee down the front of her trench coat. He apologized over and over. He even offered to pay for the cleaning. She refused. She said it was time to have it cleaned anyway.

After he admitted to being lost, she volunteered to show him where the building was located; it was down the street from where she worked. In the five minute walk, he knew he wanted to know her better. With the window of opportunity closing with each step, he asked her out to dinner. To his surprise, she accepted.

It was a blessed day. He also got the job, although he could barely stay focused during the interview. He couldn't get his mind off Annette.

They were engaged six months later and were married a year to the day at City Hall. They chose to have a simple wedding and splurge for a bigger reception. They knew financial woes put burdens on the best of marriages.

Frank was grateful for their fifteen years of marriage and four terrific children; he missed her so much.

Chapter 21

"How in the world did I end up out here?" Frank asked himself as he looked around and walked out into the backyard. The screen door slammed behind him. It was mid November and the campground was a blend of yellow, purple and red from the many sweetgum trees. A resinous aroma from the juniper trees filled the air. Frank spotted a pump to the right and a paved walkway to the left that led to what look like a small tool shed at the end of the back yard. Frank had to admit the location was serene. The crisp fall air was refreshing.

Frank had hollered at Marcus a week earlier about watching television before doing his homework. All of the girls looked at him in disbelief. He had always been the quiet one. Annette had been the disciplinarian; she believed that she had to raise her soft voice to get their attention. All he had to do was give then the look.

His hollering had been so out of character; he knew he needed a vacation. Although he had previously declined Kirk's invitation to go to the retreat, he accepted the subsequent offer. Frank shared his plans with Jerome who surprisingly agreed to come along.

On the bus ride, Jerome had confided in Frank that his wife, Alma had filed for divorce. He hadn't gone into a lot of details but had admitted that he had often neglected her. Each time she suggested a play, a movie or dinner; either he was too tired or was working overtime.

An hour into the trip, Frank was beginning to second guess himself. To get away with just guys for a week sounded great. But a retreat?

Wasn't that for ladies? Real men didn't talk about personal stuff. They just worked them out the best that they could, right?

After unloading the bus, the guys, except Frank and Jerome, headed straight to the check-in cabin. Jerome wanted to check out the lake. He was looking forward to catching some Blue Gills. Frank was having doubts, decided to look around.

There was no denying the breathtaking view!

There was a large backyard with a pump on one side and two swings on the other side. As far as the eyes could see, there were trees covered in shades of orange and gold.

Frank walked over to the swing. He twirled it around as he remembered the fun times he had with Annette and the kids in the park. He was beginning to relax; after all he had not had any time to himself since her death. Oh, how he missed his wife. This would have been heaven on earth to her, he thought, as he stepped over something left behind by, hopefully, a dog and not a bear.

Then he spotted it: An outside toilet. He had been told that it was a back-to-nature outing for the men. Not once did he think it was this far back. It was primitive enough the fact they didn't have t.v. or radio, especially on a Monday night in November. One thing for sure: He knew there would be no trips to the toilet at night. This would be one week he would find out just how much a bladder could hold.

The compound was comprised of four cabins and sat on about 10 acres of land. There was not another building for miles.

Frank looked down as he felt something on his foot. He looked down into the pop–eyes of a big green frog. "Aaaahhh," he yelled as he kicked out his leg. Relieved that it was only a frog, his heart, nonetheless, kept pounding. Frank encouraged himself, "Come on now, Frank, tough it up." As he climbed the steps of the cabin, the hairs on his neck stood out and his heart raced as he heard a howling sound coming from the woods. He was sure it was a wolf— and it seemed to be very close.

"I got a feeling we are going to run into a lot more than a few frog," Frank mumbled under his breath before heading back into the cabin.

"Good evening, guys," the director spoke, as he stepped to the front of the room. "I pray that your ride was enjoyable."

He continued. "My name is Walter; I'm the director of this retreat. If you have any complaints, suggestions, I welcome them. It's kind of late, so I know you all are tired and can hardly wait to take a bath and hit the sack."

There were some nods and agreements from the group.

The look on the director's face revealed that was the response he was expecting.

"And you can. The pump is out back to your left and seven tubs are hanging on the wall on the porch." The director was tall with little flecks of gray visible in his receding hairline. He looked fiftyish. One of men could be overheard expressing reservation about the retreat, although they'd been there less than an hour. The complainer wore a leather jacket, slacks and loafers while everybody else had on jeans, aged sneakers and lightweight jackets.

"Don't say I didn't warn you, my friend," said the guy behind him.

"Yeah, I know what you said, but I thought, I mean, I heard…."

"What?" his friend asked.

"I heard Tasha saying that the retreat is a nice get-away in a luxury resort."

"It is." His friend agreed "That is the one the ladies are attending this week. But not us guys, we want a real retreat, a back to basic, right men?"

The guys all laughed but nobody said, "Yeah."

The director continued his speech. "There are 48 of us. We will break off into groups of fours. Each group will spend the week together." The guys exchanged glances as they wondered who their roommates would be.

The director continued, "I want each of you to be prayerful that God will give you something to share that will impact the others for the rest of their lives."

They all agreed.

"Let's pray," the director instructed, "and we will be dismissed for dinner."

The dining hall was the large cabin at the end. They had a surprisingly great dinner: fresh fried blue gill, baked chicken, green beans mixed with carrots, mashed potatoes, some type of pasta and pound cake. The men found out later that the director, a chef, had cooked all of the food.

After dinner, Frank and several of the guys played Bid Whiz until late in the night. This was a time to get acquainted with each other. The official retreat would start the next day.

Frank knew a hot bath always helped him sleep well, but the thought of pumping and warming the water didn't appeal to him. He raised his arm and sniffed. Convinced that he wouldn't offend his roommates, Frank went to find his cabin.

Cabin D read the sign with an arrow pointing to the left. Frank followed the path. "D" as in DON'T STAY-LEAVE AS FAST AS YOU CAN, Frank thought, as he pushed open the door. The individual rooms were modestly furnished with a pair of bunk beds and double chests on each side. There was no closet but a cloth rack in the middle of the room. Since Frank never unpacked, even when they stayed in nice hotels, these accommodations were fine.

∗   ∗   ∗

Seven days later, Frank had to admit, that it had been a wonderful experience. For the first time in his life he'd been able to cry without feeling like a wimp. He'd been able to share what was on his heart without worrying about being judged.

As he packed to return home, he thought of the kids. He'd really enjoyed hanging out with the guys, but was looking forward to going home.

He sat his bag by the door and sat at the table. He looked around the room—a room that had been bubbling with laughter, soaked with tears, and filled with hymns the whole week was now quiet. Frank smiled as he played back the last seven days.

He had been paired with Jerome and two other guys who were totally opposite from him, yet so very much alike. From the moment they introduced themselves they had formed a bond.

Frank started the rap session by introducing himself.

"My name is Frank. I'm a... I have three daughters and a son." He had never said the word widower before. He knew he had to; he had to say it tonight. "I'm a widower."

"Matthew—married with a daughter and a beautiful grandson."

"Jerome—divorced but seeking to be reconciled."

"Hi my name is Ben—married with a teenage son and seven year old twins: a boy and girl. I didn't think so at the time but looking back, I'd have to say I was a wimp. I wanted so much to make the woman I

love happy that I didn't take my place as the head of the house in all areas. I was afraid of losing her." He forced a smile "Don't you know. That's exactly what happened. I lost her and my children for six whole years." His voice drifted off. No one said a word. The look on his face said he wasn't finished.

Silence.

The room was quiet. Everyone was reminiscing.

Jerome spoke. "I know you guys may have a hard time believing this but I was faithful the whole time. But, I was very controlling. I wanted things my way. I was always fishing or bowling. I was never interested in the things she wanted to do. I don't know what happened. I got mad and left over silly stuff. I stayed with my brother two weeks. When I came back home we talked for hours the first night. I thought everything was resolved that night, but it wasn't. The next morning she had left me a note." He chuckled, "I left her one the first time, but when she left me one, saying she needed some time to sort things out, I freaked out!!!!"

Silence.

Jerome continued. "You know, in a way, those two weeks were as traumatic as some years. God gave me a glimpse of what I'd put her through. You know what? It wasn't a pretty picture."

Silence.

"I'm sorry; I didn't mean to monopolize the conversation," Jerome apologized.

Walter insisted. "Look, take as much time as you need. This is why we are here."

Jerome started to speak and then shook his head.

Matthew, the oldest in the group asserted "You know, I've learned that if we go into a marriage with the mindset that God wants me to have one mate until death do us part, we wouldn't have so many problems. There wouldn't be so many divorces. No, not us; we go into marriage with the attitude that we are going to try to make it work for a little while; if it doesn't work out, we'll just get a different partner." He continued: "Think about it. Suppose you could only have one car for the rest of your life. How would you treat it?" he asked. They all chuckled.

"No, seriously; how would you treat your car?" He asked.

"Well," Frank began, "I know I wouldn't let the girls eat in it."

"And, I'd get an oil change every so many miles instead of waiting until the light comes on," Ben added.

"Exactly" agreed Matthew. "We would cherish it. But think about it. Our wives beg us to spend time with them doing what they like or to buy them a little 'just because' gift every now and then. We need to take responsibility for our failing marriages instead of blaming society. You hear guys bragging about their affairs and conquest and we begin to think that's what makes a real man. The truth is, it doesn't take will power to say 'yes'; that's like going down stream. But, are we able to say 'no' when there's a beautiful lady working side by side us in a small office. We smell her perfume every day and see her wearing tight sweaters. Now that's when you need some will power; no, that's when you need some God power." His voice trailed off, "In my case, I should have seen it coming, but the truth is, I was flattered." He dropped his head.

Matthew quickly reminded him, "God is a God of a second chance. He's a God of reconciliation." Jerome raised his head as his countenance lifted, "He is, isn't He?" Matthew nodded. "I know from experience."

Frank looked around the room which had been his home for only a week, but had left an impact that would last a life time.

"Hey, Frank, time to board up" a familiar voice called.

"I needed this weekend" confessed Frank, "more than I realized."

"You won't believe this. Well... yes you will. I talked to Alma this morning. Guess what? She wants us to give it another try." Jerome grinned as he explained, "I've learned my lesson. I won't be taking her for granted anymore." He dropped his bags and dug into his coat pockets. Panic instantly covered his face but quickly turned into a smile. "I forgot where I put it."

He picked up his duffel bag and eagerly opened it. He pulled out a small gray velvet box.

"Some of us went into town last night. Look what I found in the little gift shop." He opened it to reveal a beautiful pair of diamond earrings.

He was grinning ear to ear. "I know I'm going to have to brown bag it the rest of the year, but you know—the smile on her face is going to be worth it."

Sadly he confessed. "This is the first time in years I've bought her a gift. She buys me stuff all the time. You know why she says she buys it?"

Frank knew the answer to that question. He nodded "just because."

Jerome looked bemused, "yeah, right."

"Hey, Jerome, you are a barber. What can I do about this receding hairline? Is there any way I can get my hair back?" Ben asked as he walked up to the bus.

Jerome examined his head for a second. "Yeah," Jerome declared "you got to be born again."

Ben knocked his hand down. "Man, you're crazy. Get on the bus."

Chapter 22

Frank waved to the bus driver and opened the front door. He checked his watch. 12:04 a.m. He placed his duffel bag on the side of the couch and hung his jacket in the hall closet.

The time with the guys had granted him the opportunity to get other men's perspective, a time to be transparent and not feel uncomfortable about it. It had been very liberating to know he wasn't alone in the way he was feeling—about Annette's death, being a single parent, or his ambivalence about Lisa.

Frank pulled off his boots and stretched out on the couch. He dozed off thinking "there is no place like home."

The children awakened him early the next morning. As usual, they had enjoyed Grandma Kate but were happy to have him home. Each had exciting stories to share and even more questions to ask about his "wilderness experience."

After Grandma Kate left, Frank took the pipe in the bathroom sink apart. One of Lindsey's toys had become lodged in the pipe. The house was very quiet. Marcus, Angie and Lindsey played in the backyard while Sheila watched television in the living room.

The smell of burnt popcorn permeated the house.

"Something is burning!" shouted Frank.

No response.

Sheila rushed past him into the kitchen.

"Sorry, dad."

He followed her into the kitchen. "What were you watching that was so intriguing that your sense of smell was on shutdown?"

Sheila covered her nose as she pulled the burnt bag of popcorn from the microwave.

Frank noticed there were 33 minutes left on the microwave. "What did you have it set on?" he asked.

Sheila looked embarrassed. "I guess I inadvertently set if for 40 minutes instead of four."

"What were you trying to do? Burn the house down?"

Sheila was intrigued. "No, I was trying to watch the last of the program, dad. Plastic surgeons can do all kind of stuff."

"I thought we resolved that last week. You still think your lips are too large?" Frank inquired.

"No, dad, I... I mean... it's just a show."

"Honey, I know it's just a show but it deals with the weakness of people. Remember last week? They took a beautiful young lady who looked like her mom and made her look like that actress you like, that singer. Now, how do you think it made her mom feel? Honey, that show plays on people's vulnerability. Who gave them the right or authority to define what beauty is? Outward beauty is an extension of what's on the inside—not silicon, Botox or plastic surgery."

He continued: "People who are heavy want to lose weight; people who are thin wants to gain weight; blacks lighten their skin; white people tan to get darker skin. I even read where some Chinese women have surgery to make their eyes look less Asian. Honey, embrace who you are. Just as our fingerprints are unique, honey, so are each of us."

"You know, honey, there are people who change their names because they don't want a slave name. So they get an X or a Y or a Z for a last name and you know what? It doesn't link them to a single person they know; not a single person who has sown seeds into their lives. At least with their original name it linked them to at least two or three generations of family members."

He wondered whether or not he was getting through to her. "Come here, honey. Let me show you something." He beckoned for her. "Make sure you put it on four minutes this time, please."

Sheila set the microwave and followed her dad down the hall to the bathroom.

He turned her toward the full length mirror. "Look and tell me what you see."

She shrugged her shoulders.

"You know what I see?"

"What?" she asked.

He took a deep breath and grabbed her hand. "I see a beautiful young lady that looks like her mom." Sheila smiled.

"You know what else I see?"

"What?"

"I see an intelligent, fun-loving, kindhearted young lady. And you know what? I bet you her mom is smiling down on you and telling the angels, "that's my baby!"

Sheila hugged her dad. "Thank's, daddy."

"Where are you going?"

"To cut the television off."

"Dad, come here, come here, please!"

He rushed to the living room to find Sheila pointing to the television.

"Look."

On the screen was an infomercial. It was advertising a cream to get plump pouty lips.

It was confirmation.

"Thanks, dad; you're the best."

"No, it's just that I was once a kid. I know how peer pressure can be," he stated as he gave her a hug.

"Dad, can I make something to drink?" Lindsey yelled from the kitchen.

"Yes, dear, but follow the directions on the package," he reminded her.

"Dad," she yelled again.

"Yes, dear," he answered in a mock tone.

"It needs more sugar."

"Wait a minute." He whispered to Sheila. "Follow me."

She quickly followed him into the kitchen, where Lindsey was holding the sugar canister.

"It needs more sugar, Dad," she repeated for emphasis.

"Let's see what we can do. Sheila get the ice cubes for your sister, please. Lindsey, get me a glass; I think I'll have a glass with you."

Sheila knew something was up. She kept her eyes on her dad while she removed the tray of ice from the freezer. While Lindsey climbed the two steps of the kitchen stool to get a glass, Frank clanked the spoon in the sugar canister and pulled it out empty.

Sheila smiled and said, "Lindsey, pass me a glass, please." Still on the ladder, Lindsey took another glass from the cabinet.

Frank filled the glasses and waited for Lindsey to taste it. She smiled approvingly.

"Thanks, Dad; this is much better."

*　*　*

Recognizing the mailman's whistle Lindsey threw down her rope and ran from the backyard. She reached the steps as he rang the doorbell.

"Hi Leslie, you must be expecting something today," he asked as he retrieved the mail.

"My name is L-i-n-d-s-e-y!" she corrected.

"Sorry, L-i-n-d-s-e-y. Is it your birthday again, already? Do you get two birthdays a year?" he jested.

"No, I only get one. Everybody gets one. You didn't know that?" she giggled.

"Today is my birthday. I'm six. Who told you? How did you know? she asked.

"You told me yesterday and the day before and the day before that."

"You are six and I'm six. We are the same age."

"You're not six; you are grown."

"Oh, you said six; I thought you said sixty- six."

"Noooooooooo! I'm six!" she giggled.

"I'm sorry, Lindsey. I don't have anything for you but I have a certified letter. Is your dad home? He has to sign for it."

"He has to do what?"

"He has to sign…he has to write his name."

"I know how to write his name. It's F-r-a-n-k. I can write cursive; let me show you."

"Hi, Joe," greeted Frank, as he opened the screen door. The carrier stepped back and to Lindsey's disappointment handed Frank a slip to sign.

"I wanted to sign it," she sighed.

"Oh, I know. Here you go Miss Six Year Old." The carrier reached into his bag and gave her a form to sign. After he signed, Frank gave the pin to Lindsey. She quickly signed her name and proudly gave it to the carrier.

Chapter 23

Cold, wet and tired with a bowed down head, Mrs. Pauley slowly made her way upon the train platform. For the third time in a row she had to find a warm place to lay her head. Her cart filled with her belongings was safe and secure at the textile company across from the park. Whenever it rain, if Jeanette the security guard was on duty she graciously allowed her to store her cart on the lot behind the dumpster. It grieved her that Mrs. Pauley slept on the trains when there was an unused security tower with heat. Regrettably, the company had a zero tolerance for nonemployees on the premises.

As the train pulled into the station, Mrs. Pauley scanned the cars in search of an empty one. Finding one, tired and sleepy, she stepped into the train. She sat on the end seat, pulled her cap down upon her head and curled up in a fetal position. Almost immediately, she was snoring.

She jumped to her feet as her cap was snatched off her head. Laughing, a young man and two young ladies sat down across from her. Mrs. Pauley heard a snicker from behind her and spun around. A young man held his hand up as he twirled her cap around.

"Terry, right here," one of the young ladies called out as she cupped her hands. Backward and forward, they threw the cap to each other. Even thought they were teens, they reeked of alcohol.

As quick as lightening, a hammer appeared in Mrs. Pauley's hand. As she raised her arm and slowly advanced toward the young man holding her cap, their laughter turned to panic.

"Hey, lets get out of here. That old lady is crazy," yelled one of the young ladies as the train pulled into the station. Hurriedly, the three exited the train.

The young man path to the door was blocked.

Alone, the young man's voice cracked as he apologized. "I'm sorry. I was just playing. I was just having a little fun." He offered the cap to Mrs. Pauley. She didn't take it. With a desire to teach him a lesson, she squinched her eyes and glared at him.

Visibly shaken, he whimpered "I didn't mean any harm."

Mrs. Pauley had no intention of hurting anyone, no less, a kid. However, she did sense a need to teach him a real lesson.

Alone in the car with Mrs. Pauley, he looked terrified as the door opened, closed, and the train began to slowly pull off.

Again and again, the train stopped, doors opened and closed.

The young man whimpered as Mrs. Pauley glared.

Finally, the train pulled into another station, Mrs. Pauley stepped to the side. Hesitantly, the young man moved toward the door. His eyes never left the hammer.

At the door, he breathed a sigh of relief. As the train came to a grinding halt, Mrs. Pauley raised the hammer over her head, aimed for the door and threw it with all of her might.

"Ooooww!"

He hollered even thought she had purposely missed him. He bumped into the pole, reached down with one hand for his baggy pants which had dropped below his knees. In a state of panic, he pushed the partly closed doors opened and ran toward the escalator.

As the train pulled off, Mrs. Pauley noticed the platform clock. It was 1:15am. Alone, she stuck her hammer in the inside pocket of her coat. She picked up her cap and pulled it down on her head. She took her same seat, balled up in a fetal position, and in minutes was snoring softly.

*   *   *

Dr. Ahmed walked over to her desk and sat down. She checked her watch. It was 11:45. This was a sad day for her. Today, she would have to tell Mrs. Pauley that she was relocating to San Diego in two weeks. She had grown to love Mrs. Pauley's.

The doctor leaned back in her chair, chewed the tip of the pencil as she recounted the first day they'd met.

It had been a very busy Monday morning. After attending two meetings, Dr. Ahmed stopped at a small diner for coffee. Not one to waste time, she took her briefcase inside to do some work. Her secretary had called and needed some information from one of the files Dr. Ahmed had in her briefcase.

While on her way to the car, her phone had rung. She had accidently placed it inside her briefcase instead of her purse.

Dr. Ahmed had sat her purse on the bumper of the car while she retrieved her phone from the briefcase. Her secretary needed her at the office as soon as possible.

It wasn't until she reached her office that she realized she didn't have her purse. She remembered having placed it on the bumper of the car. She called the diner so someone could check. The waitress had even checked some of the other stores to see if it was returned. No one had turned in her purse.

At the end of the day, Dr. Ahmed made a mental note of the things she had to do: get replacement driver's license, vehicle registration card and report her lost credit cards.

As she stepped off the elevator, Mrs. Pauley was standing there holding her purse. She had opened it and seen her business card. She explained that it took her a long time because she had to take two buses and a train, and insisted the doctor check the contents.

All of the contents were there: the $100 her secretary had repaid, plus the $50 for the store.

Dr. Ahmed was grateful and offered her a monetary reward. Mrs. Pauley refused. Dr. Ahmed invited her to have dinner with her in the adjacent building. She refused. Dr. Ahmed was adamant about rewarding her and would not take no for an answer. Mrs. Pauley, down to less than ten dollars and feeling hunger pangs, relented. Dr. Armed was intrigued with Mrs. Pauley's determination to retain her dignity.

Dr. Ahmed was a clinical psychiatrist who had practiced over thirty years. In Mrs. Pauley, she SAW the goodness of her heart by her kind acts and HEARD the pain in her unspoken words.

As they ate dinner, Dr. Ahmed shared stories about her life, which moved Mrs. Pauley to open up about hers. Two hours later, Mrs. Pauley had committed to coming to Dr. Ahmed's office each Friday at noon just to talk.

There was a soft tap on the door.

"Come in. Please, have a seat Mrs. Pauley. Dr. Ahmed walked over to the window as Mrs. Pauley sat down.

"It's been eight months since you walked through those doors," Dr. Ahmed said as she stared out of the window.

Mrs. Pauley immediately noticed a change in Dr. Ahmed's demeanor. Dr. Ahmed typically hung her lab coat on the back of the chair; she had chosen to wear it during their meeting for the first time. Their informal meetings, devoid of the doctor/patient dichotomy, were comparable to two old friends chatting.

Dr. Ahmed turned from the window and looked intently at Mrs. Pauley. With the naked eye, everything looked the same. The red coat, and the run over sneakers were the same she had worn the first day they had met back in May. Dr. Ahmed knew, however, nothing on the inside was the same.

Dr. Ahmed squared her shoulders and announced, "It's time for you to take back your joy, your life, your happiness, and your family."

Mrs. Pauley nodded in agreement. She was eager to reunite with her family, starting with Lisa.

After an hour of chatting, Dr. Ahmed presented her with a parting gift. Each week they would end their visit with "see you next week," but not this time. For the first time they exchanged goodbyes; and Mrs. Pauley slowly made her way to the elevator.

As she stepped into the elevator, Mrs. Pauley wore a brand new navy wool coat and new gym shoes; close to her chest, she carried a tote Dr. Ahmed had given her. Inside were 2-$100 gift cards, a letter to a small Bed & Breakfast owned by one of Dr. Ahmed's cousins, and a brand new outfit for her "brand new start." Mrs. Pauley had adamantly refused the gifts until Dr. Ahmed revealed that strangers in her small hometown in India had blessed her after hearing that she was going to America.

She was simply paying it forward and she challenged Mrs. Pauley to do the same.

On the ground level, Mrs. Pauley exited the elevator and made her way across the room. As she stepped into the revolving door, she took a deep breath, knowing that as she stepped out on the sidewalk, she'd be stepping into a new life

*   *   *

Lindsey knocked on her father's door early Saturday morning. The sun had not risen; the cartoons had not come on; but Lindsey wanted to remind her father of his promise. With Sheila and Angie at Shanta's sleepover and Marcus on a camping trip with his friend J.J., Frank had promised Lindsey that they would have a Father/

Daughter Day. He'd imagined a day filled with puzzles, cartoons, miniature golf in the back yard and snacks. Unbeknown to him Lindsey had other ideas. She had the park in mind.

As Frank maneuvered the corner at the entrance of the park, he slammed on the brakes as a young boy on a bike turned the curb and fell. He missed the boy by inches. Frank's heart raced as he hurriedly exited the car. He reached the young man as he picked up his bike and dusted off his pants. He was about eight or nine.

"You didn't stop or look; you just shot across the street. Are you crazy?" Frank shouted as his heart did back flips. Although he was only going thirty on a residential street, the thought of what could have happen gripped him with fear.

"My bad," The boy responded dismissively.

Frank's fear turned to anger. "I know it was your bad, but next time it may be your behind."

The boy jumped on the bike and quickly disappeared down the street.

"Did you see that?" Frank asked as he buckled his seatbelt.

"Yep! That's Rickie. He lives on Ninety Sixth Street."

"He's going to be Rickie living on Six Feet Under Street if he keeps riding like that," Frank countered, as he shook his head still shaken from the incident.

The park, usually filled with children and adults, was practically empty. Lindsey didn't seem to notice as she headed for the sliding boards. A stretched limousine parked across from the park caught Frank's attention. He had always admired commercial drivers for their ability to drive double buses and 18 wheelers. He couldn't imagine driving such a vehicle, day to day. The chauffeur was sitting nearby on a bench.

Frank had resolved to the fact that he would miss the game at twelve. He hoped to be home in time to catch the one at 2:00. He glanced at his watch. It was 1:15. Ater sliding, swinging, climbing the monkey bar for hours; Lindsey was showing no signs of winding down.

"Push me higher, Daddy."

"Sorry, but this is high enough."

"Mrs. Pauley, Mrs. Pauley; stop Daddy; stop!"

As quickly as Frank brought the swing to a halt, Lindsey jumped out and dashed across the park. Frank was quickly in tow. An elderly, homeless-looking woman filled a water bottle and then quenched her thirst. Lindsey excitedly tapped her on the arm.

"Hi, Mrs. Pauley."

The lady turned with a broad smile.

"Hi, beautiful," she replied.

It wasn't Mrs. Pauley. Lindsey turned disappointedly to her dad.

"Daddy, I want to go home," Lindsey pouted.

The confused woman looked at Frank for an answer. "Sorry," he explained, "she thought you were someone else."

"I get that all the time. The paparazzi confuse me with some big time celebrity." She gave a hearty laugh as she sprinkled on the ground a handful of seeds for the birds.

"What's your name beautiful?" she asked squatting down.

"Lindsey"

"That's such a beautiful name."

"You have beautiful eyes," Lindsey said politely.

"Ah, that's the sweetest thing someone has said to me in years."

"We have to go, but it has been nice meeting you," Frank stated and glanced at his watch. The game would be on in twenty minutes.

"Would you like to help me feed the birds?"

Lindsey looked at her dad; he nodded.

"Sure," Lindsey answered cheerfully.

Frank walked over to a bench as Lindsey and the woman fed the pigeons and chatted. He wasn't sure which of them was giggling the most. Their laughter brought joy to his face. The woman asked Frank, after emptying the last seeds on the ground, "May I give her money for ice cream?"

He hesitated. He knew it was probably all she had but didn't want to insult her. He said, "Yes."

The woman joyfully reached in her old purse and pulled out a coin purse. She pressed a bill into Lindsey's hand and closed it up.

"Thank you," smiled Lindsey.

"I'm sorry I am not Mrs. Pauley. Mrs. Pauley is a blessed woman to have a friend like you, young lady." She turned to Frank, "May I give her a hug?" He agreed again.

"Dad," whispered Lindsey, "she smelled nice."

Frank looked back over his shoulder. The woman's clothes, although old and tattered, were very clean. Even her shoes were clean. There was something strangely familiar about her laughter. It reminded him of…. No, it couldn't be. He shook his head as he and Lindsey cut across the park.

As Frank fastened his seatbelt Lindsey handed him her money.

"Dad, keep this. I don't have any pockets."

It was a fifty-dollar bill. Frank looked back at the water fountain. The limo passed by and the chauffer blew the horn. The bird lady waved.

Frank chuckled. "You sure can't judge a book by its cover" was all he could say. He had heard the laughter many times before. It belonged to an actress from a 1960's sitcom.

*   *   *

The next day, the girls fixed a wonderful Sunday's dinner, and Frank volunteered to clean up the kitchen. He drafted Marcus to help.

While Marcus talked about his camping trip, the girls watched the movie, "The Princess and the Frog."

Around 6:00 as the sun was going down, Lindsey wanted some ice cream. She ran up stairs to get her piggy bank. She hoped Angie would take her to the neighborhood store.

Frank stopped her at the bottom of the stairs.

"No ice cream today, young lady."

"But, Dad!"

"No, but, Dad, me! You have been eating too much junk lately. You had ice cream yesterday after the park, and now you want to spend your allowance on ice cream."

"But, dad, I am hungry."

"Get an apple; there are grapes in the fridge."

"Dad, can I buy healthy stuff?"

"Sure, as long as it's healthy."

"Okay, deal," Lindsey acquiesced.

"Deal!" Frank confirmed.

They shook.

Lindsey walked out of the room singing she could buy anything she wanted as long as it's healthy. She ran back into the room.

"When I go to the store I'm going to spend all of my money on pecans because they taste g-o-o-d!" she exclaimed.

"That's fine, honey," Frank replied and smiled as Lindsey exited the room.

"But, Dad, they are 98 percent fat; I read it in my calories book," Angie protested.

"I know, honey."

Seeing his smirk, she added "Well, Isn't that defeating the purpose?"

"Nope."

"Pecans are fattening! And you are going to let her spend her whole allowance every week on pecans?"

"Yep!"

He laid his paper down and smiled; Angie looked confused.

"How much is her allowance a week?"

"Two dollar... Oh, I get it."

"Just how much you think she can buy with two dollars?"

"That's smart thinking, Dad, smart thinking," she laughed and gave him a thumb up.

*   *   *

"Dad, what is that word when some one acts like they know everything in the world." Sheila queried. "They are always trying to do things to make people like them instead of just being themselves."

"Ahhh, I'm not sure honey. Do you mean impress?"

"Yes, that's it. Impress. In school Friday Mrs. Bell read a beautiful poem to us in class. One of the girls in our class always act like she has seen every famous person in the world just because her dad works at the airport. She said she had met the author last year. But everyone knew she was lying."

"Well, how can you be sure, baby? What was the author's name?"

"The author's name was anonymous!"

They both laughed as Frank headed upstairs to change into some lounging pants.

Dad, can you help me with this game, please?" Lindsey pleaded from across the hall.

"Give me five minutes, Lindsey."

Sheila had found a great website for kindergarteners. Frank allowed Lindsey to play a half hour each evening after dinner.

"Look, Dad, these people don't have on any clothes."

"Oh, no," Frank whispered as he grabbed his jeans off the back of the chair. He'd heard of cable channels sending unapproved movie channel to neighbors. His foot became entangled in the leg of his jeans, which caused him to fall and hit his head on the end of the dresser. He stubbed his toe on the leg of the bed in his haste to get up. He hopped across the hall to the girls' room.

His heart was racing as he hoped for the best. Lindsey looked up mystified, "Daddy, you wanted to play this game really bad; you came really fast."

On the screen were two rows of stick men and women wearing job hats and helmets covered with feather, fur and scales and a row of animals wearing different kind of uniforms. The caption read: match the persons and animals with their correct covering or uniform.

Frank shook his head in relief and took a deep breath.

"Don't worry, Daddy; I'll help you. Remember, no one knows everything."

*   *   *

Angie washed a bowl of green and red grapes and sat them in the center of the kitchen table. Her siblings grabbed handfuls as they finished their homework.

"Have you noticed Dad since he got home from the trip?" Angie inquired.

"Noticed what?" asked Lindsey as Sheila and Marcus waited for her answer.

"I don't know. Maybe he and Ms. Lisa broke up," Angie answered.

"No, I know Dad likes Ms. Lisa. I overheard him talking to Mr. Kirk." Marcus said.

"You think they will get married?" questioned Lindsey.

"I think he wants to, but I think he's worried that maybe we won't accept a new mom."

"A new mom?"

"Yes, Lindsey."

She continued, "I know we all miss mom and no one can take her place in our hearts, but dad misses her the most. Dad needs a wife"

"A wife?"

"Yes, Lindsey."

"Sometimes," added Sheila, "I wish we had a mom to talk to about woman stuff."

"You do," reminded Marcus, "Grandma."

"I mean about boys, make-up and stuff."

"I know. Sometimes I wish I had a brother rather than all sisters," Marcus teased.

"I like talking to Ms Lisa. She's funny, and she knows a lot," Sheila denoted.

"That's because she works in the library and reads lots of books," Lindsey surmised.

"Mom would want dad to be married and happy. Dad is not going to be happy unless we are happy," said Sheila.

"I could be the best man," Marcus began to envision the future.

"You mean ring bearer."

"No, I mean best man. Ring bearer is for babies," Marcus insisted. "Dad always says I'm his best buddy. And the best man is always the best buddy."

"I can be the flower girl, because I'm little."

"Angie and I can be junior bride maids," Sheila went along with the speculation.

"Don't you have to be grown?" Lindsey asked.

"No, you don't." Angie answered.

"Angie?"

"Yes, Lindsey?"

"Does that mean mom is not our mom anymore?"

Angie looked at their faces. They all were waiting for her answer of encouragement.

Trying to sound mature she assured them. "No, mom will always be our mom, and she will always be with us. It's just that we will have two mommies: one in our heart; one that lives in our home."

"Daddies can have two wives, too?"

"Yes, but not at the same time. So are we all in agreement?"

"Yes, I'm in a-grease-ment!" Lindsey assented.

"Agreement," Marcus corrected.

"That's what I said."

"So while we're eating breakfast tomorrow I think we should tell him how we feel."

"How do we feel, Angie?" Lindsey wanted to know.

Chapter 24

It was the last Monday in November, with her hands thrust deep in her pockets, Mrs. Pauley walked briskly down the quiet street. Nothing was moving; vehicles nor pedestrians.

In the deepening twilight, Mrs. Pauley stopped under the light pole and stared at the small bungalow across the street. She noticed the temperature had dropped dramatically since that morning. She raised her fur-trimmed collar up around her neck. For the second time this week, she contemplated knocking on the door. For the second time, she was gripped by fear. Fear of rejection.

Click!

Unexpectedly, the street light came on. Mrs. Pauley flinched. A faint sound of a dog bark drew her attention to the window of the house next door. The curtain moved, and a figure appeared at the window.

Mrs. Pauley hastened down the street.

Chapter 25

Frank felt guilty. First, he'd gone out of town and simply told Lisa he'd be back in a week. Surprisingly, she hadn't questioned him. He had returned, yet he had not called her in two days. He knew he owed her an explanation but he needed some time to sort out his feelings. He had to be sure—for her sake, the children's sake, and for his.

He reached for the phone but paused to finish composing his thoughts. He dialed her number and rehearsed his composition. After five rings he hung up. He looked at his watch. She was usually home at this time of night.

He called again an hour later. No answer.

"Hi, Lisa, please call me," he recorded.

For the third time, Frank dialed her number.

"Hello," Lisa answered; Frank felt relieved.

"Hi, we need to talk."

Silence.

"Lisa?"

"I'm here," her tone was different.

"Are you home? May I come over?"

"Yes," she continued, "I'm home."

Confused, he entreated, "I've called you several times."

"Yes, I know."

This wasn't making sense. Was she breaking up with him? Fear gripped his heart. He didn't want to lose her. Without a doubt, he was sure that she was the one for him.

"I can meet you at the diner for coffee tomorrow morning at 7:00."

"I was hoping I could see you tonight," he pleaded.

"Not tonight," she countered with no explanation.

"Okay."

"Bye."

Bye? They had never ended a conversation with "bye." It was always, "See you later." Was he reading more into it than there was?

*   *   *

Frank checked his watch as he walked into the diner. He sat where they usually sat, near the window. Since Annette's death, he'd adjusted to his new life—going to work and raising the children. Then he met Lisa. She brought joy yet confusion; peace yet doubt.

But today was a new day and hopefully it would bring a new beginning.

Frank was perspiring as he sat looking out of the window. He felt like he was suffocating. He stretched the top of his turtleneck. He wiped his forehead with a napkin.

"Hi, my name is Karen; are you ready to order?"

"I'm waiting for someone but I will take a coffee, cream and sugar," he answered, feeling dryness in his mouth.

"Are you okay?" she asked. "You look a little flushed."

Frank wanted to say – no, I feel as though I'm about to lose the woman I love. Instead, he forced a smile and said, "I'm fine."

"Okay," she replied. It was obvious that she didn't believe him.

He was nervous as he glanced out the window. He could not lose her; he would not lose her. He knew what he had to do. For once, he had a peace about his past and an expectation about his future. He knew no one could replace Annette, but he knew clearly that Lisa wasn't a new chapter in his life but a sequel.

As he thumbed his fingers and anxiously waited for her, he looked down at his wedding band. He'd never taken it off. He smiled, pulled it off, kissed it and placed it his jacket pocket.

He sat up as Lisa slipped into the booth. Her eyes were red. It looked like she'd been crying. He reached for her hands. She momentarily hesitated yet surrendered.

"Lately, I felt like...like a puzzle with all the pieces in place except one."

Silence.

As he held her hand, his heart sank as she shook her head.

With downcast eyes, she finally spoke. "I'm confused. I mean, we've enjoyed each other. We've laughed and talked....then you shut me out, Frank."

She noticed his hands resting on the table; the ring was missing. Her eyes widened as she looked into his face for answers. Her eyes sparkled with questions but no words came from her lips.

Then, just as quickly, the smile dissipated. She dropped her head.

"Honey, what's wrong?"

"It's just," she choked back tears, "I wish Mom was here. Sometimes I just need her advice."

He scooted close, and she cried softly on his shoulders. He knew he had to go back to the park. He had to find out for sure. Was Mrs. Pauley Lisa's mom?

"Excuse me, please," Lisa said with tears in her eyes, "I have to go to the ladies' room."

"Sure."

As Frank starred out the window a small figure across the street caught his attention. It was the lady from the park. It was Mrs. Pauley. Frank called over his shoulder, "I will be right back" and dashed for the door. The waitress put her hands on her hips and looked on in disbelief.

Frank pushed open the door. The sidewalk was empty. Not one person in sight. With his head hung he walked back inside unaware of a small crowd of waitresses that had gathered.

Lisa was sitting in the booth when he returned. She looked surprised to see him coming from the outside.

"I thought I saw someone …someone I knew. Someone I'd met…" He shook his head thinking how this must sound. "Don't ask," he chuckled.

"An old flame?" she teased.

"No, no. It's a long story. I will tell you later." Frank took a sip of water. His throat was dry. Could Ms. Pauley really be Lisa's mom? She couldn't be! Or could she?

He had to get Lisa to the park. The "how" would be easy but the "when" would be a different story. He had to make sure Ms. Pauley would be there. What if she wasn't Lisa's mom? What if she was, but didn't want to see Lisa?

It was a chance he was willing to take.

"I know it's early but I was wondering would you like to go for a walk in the park?"

Lisa laughed, "Sure. When?"

"Now."

"Now, well, I guess so." They both were dressed in sweats and wearing gym shoes.

Frank was nervous. So many "what ifs" were running through his mind as they parked near the park entrance. It was a beautiful morning, not a cloud in the sky. The birds were chirping. Two squirrels were chasing each other up and down the trees. A couple of seagulls were caulking as they finished off what looked like a slice of pizza. There was a crisp and freshness in the air, yet Frank's palms were sweaty and his heart was beating up his chest. He inhaled a long breath of fresh air and hoped it would be a fresh start for Lisa.

Going to a park so early in the morning was so uncharacteristic of them, until he wondered what Lisa suspected. From time to time he caught her eyeing him suspiciously, yet she said not a word. He found himself chatting more than usual. He tried to maintain his normal disposition, but the adrenaline was in high gear.

"Let's cut across here; I want to show you something."

They walked over to the Weeping Willow and stopped. Frank's hope was dashed as he looked around. The box was gone. The only sign of what he had seen was the trampled brown grass. His mouth dropped and disappointment covered his face. Lisa noticed.

Lisa perceived that the undisclosed plan had gone awry. She asked, "Frank, are you okay? I don't understand."

He was speechless. What could he say? He was hoping she'd be here, and that it was her mom.

"Well, I mean, everything is fine"

Lisa looked at the tree. "Is this what you wanted to show me?"

Frank chose his words carefully. "Yes, this is where I wanted to bring you?" Not exactly what I wanted to show you, he thought.

Lisa nodded. "Okay. Ah…nice tree?"

She knew something was up, but what?

Frank gave her some facts about the tree he'd remembered from a story in the newspaper.

He wasn't sure Lisa bought it but he couldn't think of anything else.

She stole glances as they walked around the park and was more bewildered than ever. After 8 laps (equivalent to 2 mile), they agreed to stop for the day.

Chapter 26

It had been years since Frank had done any kind of real exercises. He felt invigorated after showering and headed down stairs to do the laundry. He filled the washer, adjusted the setting and reached for the phone.

"Hi, Kirk."

"What's up, Frank?"

"This is going to sound crazy, but I think Lisa's mom lives here," he said waiting for Kirk to make a joke.

Kirk didn't. "What makes you think that?"

"Well, I think she has been following us around town."

"What!"

"No, really. I think she was outside of Joe's Diner last night."

For over an hour Kirk listened attentively as Frank gave details to what brought him to this conclusion.

"Man, if you are right…"

"I know."

"But if you are wrong…"

"I know," Frank's voice dropped, "I know."

"What are you going to do?"

"Man, I don't have a clue."

"Keep me posted, my friend."

"Will do," he promised. The phone rung the moment he placed it on the receiver. It was Mrs. Green

"Frank, it's me."

"Hi, Mrs. Green."

President of the block club, the neighborhood watch, Mrs. Green had thwarted the burglary of two homes over the previous three years. A widow and childless, she devoted her life to the community. In addition to helping to protect her neighbors, she grew a large garden, which she learned how to do while growing up in the South. She enjoyed giving vegetables to friends and neighbors.

"I called for two reasons: First, my tomatoes did extremely well this year. I guess it was the rain. Although the squirrels have been helping themselves, I still have plenty. Send the girls over to get some."

"Man, Mrs. Green. You are right on time; I was planning to pick up some for dinner; I'm making a garden salad this evening."

"Are you cooking for the librarian?"

Nothing got past Mrs. Green; no need of lying.

"Yes, yes, I am," he admitted.

"I think that's great, Frank. Well, don't forget to send the girls over. Thanks. Bye."

"Mrs. Green? What's the second reason?"

"Oh, the mind, the mind. These days I forget a lot. Why last week I forgot to tape my favorite show. I never…"

"What's the second reason," he cut her off.

"Oh, let me see. Oh, I remember. A couple of weeks ago I saw a woman—I guess you can say homeless-looking woman—looking in your front window. At first I thought she was just passing by, but she stayed there for about 10 minutes before she left. It probably was nothing. I know sometimes, especially at Christmas, my late husband and I would drive through the neighborhoods looking through the window at the beautiful decorations. Some of us are just like that. Why, now that I think about it, it was one Saturday when the librarian was over your house."

Nothing got past Mrs. Green.

"I was going to call you but the phone rung; it was that nephew of mines begging. It slipped my mine until today." She continued, "I just wanted you to know either you have a secret admirer or a stalker on your hand."

"Let's hope it's an admirer," said Frank.

"Don't forget to send the girls over before it gets too late. You know I go to bed with the chickens."

Bed early? No way! He was sure she slept with one eye opened. She didn't miss a thing!

Mrs. Green reminded Frank of Mama Kate in every way except the gardening. The closest Mama Kate wanted to get to dirt was a mud pack in a spa.

He picked up the phone.

"Hi Mama Kate,"

"Hi Frank; how are you and my grands today?"

"Everybody is fine. I need a favor. Can you take the kids to the movies? I'm fixing dinner for Lisa."

Sure. Is 4:00 okay? And since it's the weekend, can they spend the night?" Mama Kate asked.

"Okay, whatever you say."

"Thanks."

"Frank. Can I say something?"

Sure. Of course."

Grandma Kate loved Frank and she knew he still struggled with Annette's death. Angie had confided in her a week earlier that she believed her dad wanted to marry Lisa but wouldn't because he still loved her mom.

She searched for the right words.

"Frank I don't pretend to understand life, why bad things happen to good people but one thing I do know and that is God loves us and we can trust Him. I heard someone say, at times like these we have to let our gratitude for what we had out weight our grief."

Frank nodded.

"You are a great father and you were a wonderful husband. You made my daughter very happy". She took a deep breath. I know it's hard and I know you miss her a lot."

"She was my only child; I miss her, too. But I know she wouldn't want you to live in the past. Frank, she'd want you to live your life, to love again."

Frank choked back tears.

He'd heard that before but he needed to hear it from Annette's mother.

"Thanks, Mama Kate." It was a somber moment. Mama Kate had told the truth, but the truth meant having to reaffirm that Annette was gone and would not return. A wound or sickness precedes healing, and Mama Kate had to address the wound in order to heal and find closure in her daughter's death. Mama Kate quickly changed the subject.

"What's on the menu?"

Frank announced: "Salisbury steaks, twice baked potatoes, garden salad, and chocolate cake."

"Chocolate cake or yellow cake with chocolate frosting?" she asked.

"Wait, let me get the box."

"Box?"

"Well, the picture…."

"Frank, a box cake?" she asked cutting him off, "I will make the chocolate cake and drop it off when I pick up the children."

"Thanks, Mama Kate."

"The pleasure is mine—anytime, anything for you."

At 4:02, Mama Kate was ringing the bell. Not only did she have the cake but a dozen of fresh baked rolls. Frank quickly pulled her to the side to inform her about the perfectly cut triangle pieces of bread. Mama Kate winked and walked back into the living room.

"Frank, don't forget the rolls are for Sunday's dinner not today, you hear?"

"Yes. Lindsey has already cut the bread for us. Didn't you honey?"

Lindsey nodded.

To Frank's delight, the meal met Mama Kate's approval. He had followed the recipes for the steak and potatoes to the letter and it showed. Angie had made the seven-layer salad.

After dinner, they were all excited about going to the movies until they walked out onto the porch. Lindsey took one look at Mrs. Green sitting on the porch with her poodles—Bubbles Bubbles and Curlie—and begged to stay behind.

Lindsey had asked for a puppy for her fourth birthday but Annette had a fear of dogs; it was out of the question. Frank never said anything but he really believed Mrs. Green bought the dogs for Lindsey, who often finished her chores on the weekend and asked to go next door. Mrs. Green and Bubbles were always glad to see Lindsey coming. Curlie, on the other hand, would go under the bed. Bubbles and Lindsey would sit on the couch or watch movies with Mrs. Green. Their favorite movie was Matilda. They'd watched it several times, but each time they watched it, they'd laughed as though it was their first.

Lisa came over around five. She wore a v-necked sleeveless pale blue dress. He didn't think it was possible for her to look more beautiful, but she did. She looked absolutely stunning. Her hair, usually worn straight, was in beautiful curls that framed her face.

"Frank?" she said as he stared.

"I'm sorry; please, come in," he said as he shook his head. He felt awkward as he led her to the kitchen. This was the first time they'd been alone in his home, in any home. Usually the kids were there. He knew there was safety in numbers.

The food was delicious. Lisa was impressed; it was beyond her expectation. As she cleared the table, she made an admission.

"Let me start by saying, I'm sorry I doubted your expertise in the kitchen," she kidded, "but I took the time to prepare something at home—just in case."

Frank grabbed his chest, "I'm crushed. I can't believe you doubted me?"

"But, I brought you something, so I hope this will make up for my lack of faith?" she said as she opened her bag and gave him a DVD.

"No way!"

"Yes, way. I have to confess, Marcus told me you were a big fan of Michael Jackson and that you'd never seen the Wiz."

"Yes, I am a big fan of his."

"Do you mind if we…?" he asked as he held it up.

"Perfect end to a great evening," she said as she kissed him on the lips

He checked his watch. It was 10:45. After they watched the Wiz, which he loved, they'd played Scrabble until 11:15. Lisa assured him that she wasn't Cinderella but that she wanted to be home by midnight. He agreed.

It was 12:25 when Frank returned. As he opened the back door, the aroma from the steak filled his nostrils. He smiled. It had been a wonderful evening. He reached for the cake dome but quickly changed his mind. Two slices in one evening were enough. He would have to get some roses for Mama Kate. He headed up the stairs.

Everything felt so right.

Frank checked his messages. There was one from Mrs. Green.

"Hi, Frank. Mrs. Green. Sorry to call you so late. Lindsey and Bubbles played in the backyard for hours. We all fell asleep watching Matilda. Just wanted you to know she's fine. I will bring her over in the morning. Good night."

Mr. and Mrs. Green had been married over sixty years. With no children, they had been inseparable, and she had taken his passing very hard. The girls started spending more time next door, so, as Lindsey put it, "Mrs. Green would laugh and be happy again."

That night Frank had a dream.

He was at some kind of family gathering. All of his children were there. Grandma Kate was among the guests seated at a long table filled with plenty of delicious food. A huge birthday banner was hung from the ceiling. Some of the guests were eating; others were standing around talking and laughing.

Frank was playing Bid Whiz; Annette was his partner. The call was on Frank to bid his hand. He wasn't comfortable.

Annette looked into his eyes and said to him, "No matter what; you got to play your hand."

Frank woke up with a great peace. A weight was lifted off his shoulders.

By nine o'clock the next morning, Frank had finished the laundry and mowed the yard. Lindsey was in her room coloring. Mrs. Green had sent her home with a stack of coloring books and a box of crayons.

After showering, he sat on the edge of the bed, placed his clutched hands behind his head and laid back. He stared blankly at the ceiling.

"Dad, my friend is at the door," Lindsey bellowed, as she ran down the hall.

"Lindsey, I told you to never open the door," he scolded.

"I didn't, dad," she answered as he rushed passed her; "I saw her out of the window."

Frank opened the door. He expected to see Tenille, one of Lindsey's classmates who lived three houses down and visited her grandparents each weekend. They often jumped rope and played hopscotch on the sideway together.

Frank was astounded; he couldn't believe his eyes. He couldn't help looking from her head to her feet. A neatly dressed woman with her hair pulled back in a ball, with trembling hands stood in front of him. She wore black flats that looked new. The transformation was amazing. The only sign of the old Mrs. Pauley was those piercing eyes and the crescent scar.

Mrs. Pauley spoke first—"May I come in?"

"I'm sorry; sure. Come in, Mrs. Pauley, and have a seat." he motioned. She sat on the edge of the couch as Frank chose the chair directly in front of her. Lindsey broke the silence as she sat next to Mrs. Pauley. "I love your nail polish."

Mrs. Pauley smiled and looked down at her perfectly manicured nails.

Frank hadn't said a word. He could hardly believe his eyes.

"Lindsey, will you please bring a glass of water for Mrs. Pauley?'

"Sure; be right back," came the quick response.

"Lisa is my daughter," Mrs. Pauley said. She expected Frank to be surprised. He wasn't.

"I know," he replied.

Mrs. Pauley looked surprise. She continued. "I miss her so much but I'm afraid she may not want any part of me."

Frank listened.

"I've missed so much of her life." She paused then added, "but I'm better. I'm well, now."

So many questions raced through his mind but Frank knew this was a delicate situation. He had to let her lead. So he waited and waited.

Lindsey stared into Mrs. Pauley's face. "You look nice; your face is so clean," she said as she gave her the glass of water.

"Lindsey!" called Frank.

Mrs. Pauley smiled, 'Thank you."

She knew the transformation was amazing. She had hardly recognized her own self in the mirror. She would have to thank Dr. Ahmed again for all of her help, including picking out the outfit.

Lindsey looked sad as she scooted closer to Mrs. Pauley. "I wish you were one of my grandmas, so I could visit you like Tenille visits her grandma and grandpa."

Mrs. Pauley smiled at Lindsey and then looked at Frank, "I wish you were my granddaughter, too."

"You want to see my new doll? Lindsey asked. Without waiting for an answer, she ran upstairs to get it.

Mrs. Pauley continued. "The only thing I had was a picture of the two of us. Then, I lost it. I was at Joe's Diner one day when she came in. I knew immediately it was her. It was a prayer answered. So, I started following her. She looked so sad each time, but I was afraid seeing me would just make it worst."

Mrs. Pauley smiled. "Then one day I saw you all go into the diner. I watched from the window. Then, I knew she was happy. You are the one for her."

Frank listened but he was still puzzled. "But how did you know where I lived?"

Embarrassed, she fidgeted with her hands. "One day you left your car window half down. I looked at your registration card and got your address."

Frank recalled the incident.

One of the children had spilled milk on the floor of the car. Although they tried to clean it up, they didn't clean under the floor mat. Frank had left the window down to get rid of the stench.

When they returned to the car, they noticed the glove compartment open and immediately thought someone had been in the car. However, since the change in the cup holder hadn't been disturbed, Frank assumed someone had failed to close it securely.

Frank's mind went from wondering about how she discovered his address to the purse he had found in the park. He excused himself and hurried upstairs. He jumped out of the way as Lindsey rushed pass him with an armful of her dolls to show Mrs. Pauley.

As he pulled the coin purse from the closet he could hear Lindsey telling Mrs. Pauley about Bubbles.

The phone rang.

"Hello."

"Hi, Frank, you will never believe this," Lisa started, "one of the neighbors from my old neighborhood said she saw my mom a couple of weeks ago. She said that she was on the bus…but…she is sure it was my mom. I want to go back to the neighborhood and look. Does that sound silly?"

"No, not at all."

Silence.

"Are you okay" Frank asked.

"Yes—more than ever. The day you proposed was the happiest day of my life. But, I know, when I see my mom that will be the happiest day of my life," she giggled. She asked, "Can a person have two happiest days?"

"You know. I think you can."

"Are you busy? Can I come by for a cup of coffee and to talk?"

Frank hesitated.

"If it's a bad time…

"No. It's not. Sure."

It's perfect timing, he had wanted to say.

Frank had to think fast. He called his neighbor.

"Mrs. Green, I need a favor."

He explained what he needed, and she agreed.

"Thanks, Mrs. Green. I owe you." Frank hung the phone up and walked to the top of the stairs and waited. He counted "5, 4, 3, 2, 1.

The phone rang as planned.

"Get the phone, Lindsey" Frank shouted.

"Hello. Hi, Mrs.Green. Sure. I'll ask daddy. Dad, can I go over Mrs. Green's house? She made fresh cinnamon rolls."

"Yes, and please bring me one."

"Mrs. Pauley, can you go with me so you can see Bubbles?" Lindsey asked. "He's the best dog in the whole world."

Hearing the opening and closing of the back door, Frank descended the stairs. He looked out of the window as Lisa pulled into the driveway.

Knowing he had only a few minutes before Lindsey and Mrs. Pauley would return, Frank didn't waste time.

"Lisa, come, sit here, please," he beseeched, as he grabbed her hand and led her to the couch.

"Are you okay? Are the kids okay?" she asked as she sensed his urgency. Something was different.

Frank nodded. "Everything is fine." He didn't know how to tell her that her mom was next door. He didn't know how to break the news. So, he just said it.

"Your mom is here!" he informed her.

"Yes, I told you that someone saw her in the old neighborhood. Who told you that they saw her?"

"No. I mean she is here."

"Here?"

"Well, no, not here, HERE, but next door here?"

Lisa looked even more confused.

Frank took a deep breath.

"Honey, let me explain."

He started from the beginning: the day in the park, the picture in the coin purse, the opened glove compartment, all the way up to the knock on the door.

Lisa sat enraptured and listened.

"Can we go next door?" she asked as he finished.

They heard the back door open.

"Here are your cookies, daddy. Mrs. Green sent you a lot," Lindsey announced as she and Mrs. Pauley walked into the living room.

"Hi, Miss Lisa," Lindsey spoke, "This is my friend, Mrs. Pauley. She's very nice."

Lisa eyes filled with water as she placed her hand on her heart.

Frank beckoned for Lindsey.

"Oh, Mrs. Green sent these to you, Dad."

Thanks. Bring them into the kitchen, please."

"Here, Dad, I want to…"

"Lindsey!"

She followed her father into the kitchen. "Why is Miss Lisa and Mrs. Pauley crying, Daddy?"

"It's, 'why ARE they crying?'"

"I don't know." Lindsey threw up her hands.

"Let's go thank Mrs. Green for the cookies, baby."

Lisa and Mrs. Pauley stood speechless. Each struggled to find words.

Mrs. Paula spoke first. "I am so sorry. I should have been there for you. I let you down…"

Lisa rushed into her mom's arms and they cried together. As they sat on the couch, Mrs. Pauley tried to explain.

Lisa shook her head. "Please. Not today. Just hold me. You don't know how I've long for this moment."

Mrs. Pauley nodded. "Yes, yes. I do."

Lisa fell into her mother's arm as they savored the moment. There were no words—just a sweet peace as they each relived the years they'd spent apart.

After about an hour Lindsey told her dad that she wanted some water. The truth was, curiosity had gotten the best of her. Lindsey entered the kitchen and passed the sink. She quietly cracked the door to see what was going on in the living room.

Mrs. Pauley heard the door squeak.

"Lindsey, come here please."

Lindsey knew eavesdropping was wrong. She apologized. "I'm sorry."

"Honey, that's okay. Lindsey, I want you to meet my daughter."

"Where?" Lindsey asked as she looked around the room.

Lisa giggled, "Lindsey, Mrs. Pauley is my mom."

Before Lindsey could speak, Frank walked into the room. The look on Lisa's face warmed his heart. He picked Lindsey up.

"Honey let's go upstairs; I'll explain."

Within minutes Lindsey came charging back down stairs as Frank followed.

"I have a question and Daddy has a question. You go first, Dad," Lindsey instructed.

With a military salute, Frank answered, "Yes, sir." Frank turned to Mrs. Pauley "May I have your daughter's hand in marriage?"

Before she could answer, Lindsey asked Lisa, "Can your mama be my grandma?"

Mrs. Pauley and Lisa answered in unison—"Yes!"

Epilouge

Soft jazz music played in the background. The banquet hall was small but elegantly decorated. There were ten tables covered with pink tablecloths. Each held a beautiful crystal vase filled with pink and white carnations.

Soft jazz music played in the background as the guests slowly made their way inside.

Because of the unexpected snow, the wedding was starting an hour late. In the dressing room, Lisa stood by the bay window. She looked down at her wrist and smiled.

She wore something old; a charm bracelet with a picture of her mom and dad, her wedding dress was new and Lindsey had loaned her pearl earrings.

The snow covered lawn glisten as the bright sun rays streamed down.

A hand gently rested on Lisa's shoulder. Without turning, she knew it was her mom.

"Mom, I didn't think it was possible to be this happy."

The organist began to play.

"It's time, honey."

Lisa turned and reached for her mom's hands. Her mom was smiling. Lisa had seen that smile, before.

About the Author

Catharine has been married to Thomas Ingram for thirty nine years. They have three children; Michael, Michelle and Derandel.

Catharine Ingram was born in Shaw, a small rural town in the Mississippi Delta. She has always enjoyed reading and writing short stories.

CatharIne Ingram
P.O.Box 43082
Chicago, IL 60643
USA
or e-mail me at gmcat50@yahoo.com